ELEMENTS OF SOUND

This book is part of an ongoing collaboration between HeartFire Productions, Albion-Andalus, and the related family network of Worldchangers Organization affiliates. HeartFire Productions is a multimedia production house for platforming conscious creative content and bringing visions to life. Worldchangers Organization for Inner World Peace is an interdisciplinary 501(c)3 nonprofit, international movement, and interspiritual school. We are dedicated to the vision of a new paradigm, where people live more consciously and sustainably, in harmony with each other, nature, the cosmos, and themselves. Our Two Pillars are Inner Work for Global Change and Global Work for Inner Change. Our Eight Limbs holistic education initiatives include Sanctorum Ecovillage, HeartFire Festival, Hermes Academy, and more.

Learn more at: worldchangers.us

PRAISE FOR *ELEMENTS OF SOUND*

"This is not just a book, it's an experience. Well-written, thought provoking, educational, enlightening, fascinating—the list goes on. 'Full-spectrum' is a perfect way to describe it. *Elements of Sound* is a book within a book, a masterpiece of literary art on the subjects of sound and consciousness. This is certainly a book to be read again and again."

— Kathy Lord,
Co-Founder/Managing Director, Music That Heals

"Congratulations on *Elements of Sound*. I particularly appreciate the emphasis on a musical life centered in awareness and flow. There are many life lessons throughout the book."

— Chris Azzara, Professor of Music Teaching and Learning, Eastman School of Music

"A comprehensive overview, not only of basic elements of music, but also of spirituality and metaphysics and how they all interact. There is no end to learning, and I suspect that I will continue to return to this wonderful compendium for more insight into what I know and what I don't know about sound and consciousness."

— Peter Blum, Hypnotherapist and Sound Healer

"Adrian DiMatteo is a gifted musician, theoretician, and dedicated spiritual practitioner. *Elements of Sound* is where these three aspects of his being come together in an exploration of sound and consciousness."

— Netanel Miles-Yépez, Pir of the Inayati-Maimuni Order

ELEMENTS OF SOUND

A FULL-SPECTRUM EXPLORATION OF SOUND AND CONSCIOUSNESS

Adrian DiMatteo

Albion
Andalus
Boulder, Colorado
2023

*"The old shall be renewed,
and the new shall be made holy."*
— Rabbi Avraham Yitzhak Kook

Albion-Andalus Inc.
P. O. Box 19852
Boulder, CO 80308
albionandalus.com

Design and composition by Albion-Andalus Books

Cover design by Cassie Luzenski (cassieluzenski.com)

Cover illustration: *Waves*, Maestro Manuel Rufino

Interior graphics designed by Hilal Özçelik (hilalozcelik.com)

ISBN: 978-1-953220-32-5 (Paperback)
ISBN: 978-1-953220-33-2 (Hardcover)

Manufactured in the United States of America

DEDICATION

This book is dedicated to Maestro Manuel Rufino, who has helped open so many doors in hearts and minds throughout the world. I am eternally grateful for him serving as a bridge between modern culture and ancient knowledge. Without elders and wisdom keepers to teach and share these living traditions, we would be without a compass, left to recover from ignorance what our ancestors sacrificed so much to preserve. In his own words:

*"This knowledge has been passed on
from one generation to the next,
from teacher to student, from lips to ear,
but in reality, most of the teachings
are passed on in silence, directly."*

CONTENTS

FOREWORD

Elements of Sound requires the reader to suspend not only disbelief, but also systems of belief. To receive it fully, detach from everything you think you know and simply drink the book, sip it in, chew on it, digest it. The text itself is a psychoactive compound. If you read it well, your heart and mind will change and expand by the time you finish. Pay attention to the meaning between the lines, the transmission in the empty space beyond the words and letters.

Adrian DiMatteo is a practitioner-scholar. This fact is of the utmost importance, because it endows his perspective with holism and multidimensionality. It puts him in the unique position of—not only being *able* to write this book—but ultimately *needing* to, for the sake of humanity's evolving awareness about sound and its importance. As *Elements of Sound* demonstrates—vibration is multidimensional by nature. Only someone with a multifaceted, experiential understanding of sound can do justice to the topic; a practitioner-scholar who has achieved an integral view.

Such intimate knowledge is called 'gnosis,' or, according to the Sufis, '*dhawq*,' which is the Arabic term for 'tasted' truth—the interior experience which leads to faith. Hidden and yet self-evident, this source of inner-knowing cannot be proven and yet has no need to prove itself. Despite the ineffable nature of internal experience, some authors are able to transmit their own meditations through the poetic power of language. In the opening verse of the *Tao Te Ching*, Lao Tzu acknowledges that the 'true way,' cannot be spoken and yet he proceeds to speak about the Tao with incredible precision throughout the following 81 verses of the book.

DiMatteo is able to articulate profound insights to others, making *Elements of Sound* a highly relevant and applicable text for anyone interested in the relationship between sound and consciousness. Both spiritual seekers and students of music will find an oasis of inspiration in his work.

Scientific materialism and separatism divorce mind from matter, self from other, world from psyche. Modern Western society's dominant paradigm of scholarship tends to sterilize and isolate observation and data analysis, without placing sufficient value on participatory experience. However, quantum physics suggests that it might not be possible to divide subject from object, and that both interdependently arise from an intelligent mystery. *Elements of Sound* invites the reader to realize their active role as a perceiver-creator in the world of sound.

Ancient spiritual disciplines emphasize a full-spectrum approach to learning (and unlearning). *The Kybalion* cautions readers to beware of one-sidedness, reminding them that the blade of truth is always double-edged. In Buddhism, "contemplative education" requires the cultivation of wisdom, rather than mere memorization of information. To that end, both intellectual study *and* experiential practice are coupled with reflection and integration.

As a practitioner-scholar, DiMatteo has precisely this type of approach to sonic studies—bridging worlds and connecting paths. He lives it through his actions with deep care for his art, engages rigorous intellectual study and embodies the multidimensionality of the topic. DiMatteo serves as a music educator, sound healer and retreat facilitator. He has apprenticed directly with global traditions under the guidance of elders and lineage-holders, which enrich and inform the content of this book. Furthermore, as an international performing and recording artist trained at the Eastman School of Music, DiMatteo has an advanced knowledge of many genres, instruments, techniques and theoretical systems of music.

Such a comprehensive combination of training and experience in the field of sonic studies is quite rare. For DiMatteo, this work is not only a vocation, but a life path, leading both author and reader towards greater union with the elements of sound.

Yasha S. Wagner
Founder / CVO
Worldchangers Organization

Author's Note

As I began writing this book, I confronted doubt. I questioned my understanding and the validity of this contribution. There are many books discussing the science, philosophy and spirituality of sound, meditation and healing from various perspectives. Those influential texts, both ancient and modern, have been essential to my process and I would recommend them to anyone seriously interested in the nature of consciousness where it intersects with vibration, meditation and healing (they are referenced throughout this book for those who wish to study further).

Furthermore, I was caught in an esoteric dilemma epitomized by the biblical axiom, "there is nothing new under the sun."[1] Virtually everything I know (aside from certain direct, experiential insights), I have learned from teachers and elders who pass their wisdom in ways both spoken and silent. Who am I to assert anything? How could I contrive to offer ideas alongside Lao Tzu, King Solomon, Buddha or even a certified scientist? This is not 'my' knowledge, as I stand on the shoulders of giants.

Nonetheless, I embrace that I *do* have a unique perspective, and am deeply engaged in the science and spirituality of sound. I underwent rigorous musical training at the Eastman School of Music for nearly a decade of my life, and I have traveled the world engaging with indigenous cultures and ancient musical traditions. At the same time, I've extensively studied writing and philosophy. As a sound therapist, I have worked in settings as intimate as a hospice bedroom. My experiences living in intentional communities and working with a vast network of teachers and practitioners of many modalities have given me a broad perspective on what healing and meditation mean to different people.

It is my intention that this book provide not only practical information about using sound in daily life as a tool for meditation and healing, but also a deeper context—to inspire you to explore your own ancestral music and stories, and to recognize the connection of all people through the shared teachings that unify world faiths. This includes scientific and esoteric doctrines and methods.

The intentional use of sound can greatly aid people on the journey to inner peace, which is essential for healing and understanding. It is my prayer that this book helps bring forth harmony in the world. May it inspire peace within you. It is already within you. May it help you to remember.

INTRODUCTION

Sound is an integral aspect of our lives and a fundamental component of creation. In terms of vibration, sound is audible to us within a very narrow range. Considering the comparatively vast auditory spectrum of other lifeforms, we know that more sonic information exists throughout the universe than we physically hear.[2] Nonetheless, that which we *do not* hear is equally important to understand to gain a fuller picture of sound.

Sound occurs when a force stimulates energy to vibrate. Anything that vibrates produces sound (even atoms emit *phonons*, the sonic equivalent of photons). Sound propagates via mechanical pressure waves (measured in frequency, amplitude and wavelength) which displace particles of matter. Therefore, sound physically impacts the environment, interacting with objects down to the atomic and quantum levels.

Beyond this, sound is a primary means of communication— through words, internal dialogue, music and other signals such as sirens and alarms. Auditory cognitive processes affect our emotions, and are equally capable of bringing peace and understanding as they are anger and confusion. For this reason, one who wishes to find harmony within does well to investigate the principles of sound.

The "Elements of Sound" are its underlying, universal mechanisms. We are familiar with volume, wavelength, tempo (speed) and tone as aspects of sound and music. Like levers of an intricate machine, these and other features of sound can be adjusted to produce an infinite array of forms. The diversity of music and language around the world speak plainly to sound's creative potential.

There is seemingly no end to the words human beings will write and say to each other. We fill libraries with philosophies, theories and methods. We compose endless works of art, attempting to convey our deepest sentiments. The catharsis of the creative process is known even to a child who sings and dances alone when no one is watching.

This book is intended for both non-musicians and musicians alike—although I consider such labels arbitrary, since sound and music are as integral to the human experience as breathing and thinking. I have made an effort to include perspectives from modern and ancient spheres of human legacy—science, philosophy, art and spirituality. Each of these contributes indispensable knowledge to the holistic understanding of sound.

A rabbi once told me, "We do not say there is only one God. We say that God IS one." The symbol on the cover of this book is the astrological sign of Aquarius. Among its many interpretations are this: science and spirituality are parallel lineages. The two need not conflict. It is a symbol of harmony. It is also a symbol of the sine wave. Both light and sound travel in waves; distinct yet inseparable. They are two aspects of one and the same universe.

Everyone prays in their own language,
and there is no language that God does not understand.

— Duke Ellington

Many wisdom traditions tell us that water is life, and so Aquarius (the 'water-bearer') also speaks to this elemental truth. Our bodies are largely composed of water in a proportion similar to the planet itself. *As above, so below.*[3] Science and spirituality agree that clean water is essential to health. Additionally, Aquarius is associated with the element air and the mind itself. Equally essential to life are clean air and a clear mind.

Vibrations travel through both water and air. These mediums may carry pollutants, but pollutants can be purified. If we consider purification only on the physical level, we ignore our capacity to clean our minds of disharmonious structures as well. False beliefs, animosity, arrogance and fear are no less real than protons, neutrons and electrons. There are many unseen forces that play vital roles in our lives. Just because some information is irrelevant to one science does not make it irrelevant to another. There is science that studies consciousness, and spirituality that incorporates science.

If there is any theory to be found here, it is that sound is simultaneously given and received. Sound and silence—expressing and listening—are two halves of the same coin. With awareness and intention, the creative power of vibration can be harnessed for physical, mental, emotional and spiritual purposes, whether for meditation, healing, entertainment or mundane technology.

Society is an orchestra of individuals, as the universe is an orchestra of infinite vibrations. Who can say what is dispensable or indispensable in the cosmic ecosystem? Who has the authority to decide what music is good or bad? Perhaps through this study—which is first and foremost a personal exploration—you will come to understand something about harmony: the application of wisdom with a practice of acceptance and compassion toward oneself and others.

Sometimes a mind cannot learn until it has first unlearned. Begin by clearing the cluttered hard-drive.

1. Sit upright with good posture, or comfortably as you are. Feel that your body is balanced and aligned.

2. Allow your eyelids and all facial muscles to relax completely.

3. Take a long, slow and steady inhale through the nose.

4. Exhale slowly through the nose, releasing tension from your entire body, including mental effort and emotional sensations.

5. Repeat three or more times, allowing thoughts to dissipate. Relax your entire being more deeply with each breath.

I invite you to silence, the blank canvas where sound emerges.

Part I

The Physics and Metaphysics of Sound

I

Silence: The Birthplace of Sound

The mother of sound is silence.

— *Tito la Rosa*

Silence, like the symbol 0, is an elusive principle. As darkness cannot be seen, silence cannot be heard, much less discussed. At best, our words echo the indescribable, like dust cast in the air to reveal the light beam of a projector. The nature of silence is not defined by what we say *about* it, but rather how we *experience* it through contrast. Silence exists in a sonically saturated universe and is therefore *relative* to sound.

When was the last time you heard *nothing*?

Sound and light permeate the inner and outer world. Subjective experience is perceived *directly* and can only be verified internally. No matter how we attempt to document or explain our perceptions and experiences to others, the inner life is distorted in translation. How do you describe an emotion? How do you put a sensation into words?

To this point, art has been a primary means for humanity to express the ineffable. A great deal of life's work is an individual process of integrating and transcending dualities of self and other, internal and external, birth and death, right and wrong, sound and silence. This is partly why science and spirituality often find themselves at odds. Empirical science generally attempts to understand the world through the physical senses (material, quantifiable, outwardly observable, etc.) while spirituality engages with energy on metaphysical planes, without requiring another to verify its observations.

Simply by existing with awareness, the inner world presents a complex interface of sensations and perceptions. This is true of both dreaming and waking life. Consciousness is a lens of awareness through which we view reality. That which is unconscious does exist, but without awareness. Absolute silence is already in coexistence with infinite forms and vibrations that manifest on a daily basis (thoughts, emotions, bodily sensations, physical phenomena, etc.).

The act of perceiving requires us to be in relationship with time, space, energy and vibration. Unordered vibration, we call chaos. Ordered vibration, we call the laws of nature. Gravity, the speed of light and the speed of sound are a few *relatively* stable attributes of our universe (although they may not be inherent to other dimensions or universes). Some ascribe these ordered principles to God, or a sentient creative force. Others view them as natural or mechanical processes (such as the laws of physics, cause and effect, etc.). Ultimately, religious, spiritual, philosophical and scientific theories have been unable to pinpoint the fundamental origin of the universe or construct a fully unified theory of reality. The mentalities which come closest are perhaps those which embrace that we may never arrive at total knowledge.

Theories are closed systems of logic which attempt to put the universe in a rational box. While a computer can produce an infinite array of projections, the human mind is aware that the interface of a computer is generated within the computer itself, and is thereby limited by its logic. In that sense, we are also limited by our own logic. How can a machine produce anything other than what it was designed to create? Meditation is a way of decoding and reprogramming consciousness. It allows us to learn and unlearn, receive and process new information in a non-linear way. Perhaps for a moment in meditation or a lucid dream, one is able to step out of the rational box and experience reality from another perspective. Our potential capacities as human beings are generally as underdeveloped as early computers compared to modern machines.

From a biological perspective, human beings are engineered with particular capacities for sense perception. Like musical instruments, our organs of perception are tuned to filter and process specific ranges of frequencies. As an eagle's eye is designed for aerial pursuit, or a bat's sonar (echolocation) to fly in darkness, the human being experiences life according to certain physiological and cognitive properties.

Light and sound spectrums extend far beyond what we see and hear directly, yet this does not exempt us from experiencing the effects of those vibrations in other ways. Infrared light, ultraviolet rays and radio waves are only a few examples of apparently invisible, inaudible spectrums that have a tremendous impact on our bodies, and which can be harnessed for many purposes. Today, science is introducing terms like 'dark matter' to account for significant portions of the unseen universe.

A camera is an engineered eye which detects things the naked eye cannot see, allowing us to visibly render such phenomena as night vision or heat-mapping. Astronomers point their telescopes to the darkest part of the sky to reveal that light is present. Just as the eyes acclimate to darkness, ears acclimate to silence. Polarities are relative, not absolute, enabling perception through contrast.

> What happens when you stare at the sun?
> It burns. But everyone wants to see light.
> And darkness? Look at it. You begin to see
> light that doesn't burn —
> a gentle spectrum, quiet and still.
> Nothing to be afraid of.
> But light? Watch it rightly.
> So does sound deafen
> while silence opens you to hear
> subtler things.

To the Mayan people, 0 (zero) does not mean 'nothing.' 0 is a seed, as its shape suggests. Within it lies the potential of creation, just as silence implies the potential of sound, and darkness the potential of light. These polarities are two sides of the same coin.

In a dualistic way of seeing things, it appears that opposites never touch. But in truth, both belong to the same spectrum, which is infinite. One may approach but never reach either end of this gradient. Loud and soft, fast and slow, high and low, sound and silence—these extremes operate on the same principles of relativity, contrast and interdependence.

A sculptor carves a block of stone to reveal the figure within. In the uncarved stone, its potential is latent, unborn until the artist determines what shall be made of it. Likewise, a musician (whose medium is sound) selects and combines frequencies to form a composition. So too does a painter decide which colors to harmonize, or a chef which ingredients to pair.

> *There is no art without intention.*
>
> *— Duke Ellington*

The place from which these artistic creations are born, the influences which inspire them and the principles which govern them are to be discovered through the process of mastering not only what to use, but what *not* to use. Equally important to the presence of one is the *absence* of the other. Balance is achieved with discrimination. Silence serves the music. Emptiness serves the canvas. Simplicity serves the dish.

> *I always listen to what I can leave out.*
>
> *— Miles Davis*

Silence is never lacking, even in the presence of sound. Not only what is heard, but what is *not* heard allows space for us to perceive what has been chosen at the exclusion of all else.

In the Torah, no two letters can touch. If they do, the entire rendering is invalid and must be redone. This is because, according to tradition, the White Torah is written in the negative space between the words. One must not encroach upon that boundary. It is a teaching to be revealed when one is ready to understand, hence the phrase 'read between the lines.'

A full cup cannot be used, a full hand cannot receive and a mind full of preconceptions is not open to understanding that which contradicts its assumptions. The artist must constantly balance these elements of giving and receiving, learning and teaching, observing and responding, filling and emptying. The principles of Yin and Yang are ever-present.

Vibration is characterized by motion. Total stillness (emptiness or nothingness) implies a lack of vibration. The ancient Hermetic Principle of Vibration declares, "Nothing rests; everything moves; everything vibrates." Modern physics—despite its many uncertainties and incongruities—appears to universally agree that vibration is a fundamental attribute of reality.

Focusing vibration yields powerful results. Humanity harnesses energy in many ways, channeling sources from nature such as water, wind, fire or solar energy, gravity, magnetism, etc., to generate electricity. Laser technology accomplishes this with a high degree of precision. We have also realized the immense energy stored within particles. As atomic science reveals, vibrations are not only channeled externally, but released from the inside.

There is stability and steadiness inherent to focus, like an archer on horseback. As the horse bolts across the earth, the archer must maintain equilibrium in order to aim accurately. Even in motion, stillness is present.

One who works with sound must also develop this capacity. A violinist steadies the bow. A singer sustains intonation and controls tremolo and vibrato (fluctuations in volume and pitch). A percussionist plays a consistent beat without speeding up or slowing down. This is stillness inherent to motion.

I once spoke with an elder from an initiatic tradition about a spiritual dilemma I was having. I was considering my life and mission as an artist, and what it means to be a musician in the world.

I work with sound. Music is a limited term. Sound encompasses melody, harmony, speech, thought and a universe full of vibrations. The teachings of many wisdom keepers advocate to observe silence.

"Is music a karmic attachment? Is it a pleasurable distraction?" I asked him. "Should I renounce it and retreat to a monastery somewhere to focus on my inner life in silence and meditation?"

He looked at me firmly. "There is no sound without silence. There is no darkness without light. It is not about being silent, but as you *approach* silence, you begin to hear the sound *in* the silence."

No hay sonido sin silencio. No hay oscuridad sin luz.

— *Maestro Domingo Dias Porta*

I am still integrating these words, but I realized in that moment, he was telling me not to deny who I am, not to abandon my calling, but to move towards inner silence even as words and songs pass through me.

The mirror and the object of reflection begin to merge:

Live in joy, in love, even among those who hate.
Live in joy, in health, even among the afflicted.
Live in joy, in peace, even among the troubled.
Look within. Be still. Free from fear and attachment,
know the sweet joy of the way.

— *Gautama Buddha (The Dhammapada)*

Sound and silence are always dancing, enacting the hermetic principle of polarity. Each sine wave has its peak and valley. The spaces between notes are as important as the notes themselves.

Everything is dual; everything has poles;
everything has its pair of opposites;
like and unlike are the same;
opposites are identical in nature, but different in degree;
extremes meet; all truths are but half-truths;
all paradoxes may be reconciled.

— *The Kybalion*

In meditation, as we approach stillness, we sensitize ourselves to subtler vibrations. Everyday sounds become pronounced—a drop of water, the hum of a refrigerator, someone talking in the street. We sense irritation in the physical body, urged to itch, scratch and shift in our seats. Approaching silence and stillness doesn't mean that sound ceases to be, or that reality grinds to a halt and nothing exists anymore. Rather, we gain access to deeper layers of conscious experience. The external focus may be exchanged for the internal until both are merged in a non-binary mode of experiencing *presence*. In this space, we can hear what Maestro Domingo Dias Porta referred to as "the sound *in* the silence."

One benefit of meditation comes through a sense of expansion, beyond the limited way we have of experiencing the world, beyond temporary suffering, beyond egocentric fears and assumptions about life. We come to see our blind spots.

Now let us hear our deaf spots. As the mind chatters away, observe it, simultaneously silent while thoughts ramble on like clouds drifting across an endless blue sky, gradually dissipating until one is left with a calmer, more patient, present and less attached mind.

Practicing sound meditation for oneself or facilitating it for others essentially serves this process, providing an atmosphere in which a distracted mind is held by vibrational forms that do not require analytical, rational or intellectual understanding.

Remember yourself as a child. Who was it that had those experiences? What holds those memories? Your body has changed; it is larger now. Your voice has changed; it is deeper. Your perceptions have shifted as your mind constantly recontextualizes itself with new information. Nevertheless, there is something essential to *You*, an unbroken stream of consciousness, an observer of all you've experienced from then until now. This is the silent one, the still one, the eternal one. Behind the veil of infinite forms is the essentially formless—the blank canvas on which all is projected.

There are two ways to keep silence.
One is to keep silent totally, the other is to know how to talk.

— Maestro Manuel Rufino

Many creation stories from around the world speak of the origins of the universe through the generative Word. The Torah (Old Testament) of the Jewish and Christian faiths put it this way in the book of Genesis: "And God said, 'Let there be light,' and there was light." This account suggests that creation was in some sense 'spoken' into being, or that sound preceded light. Considering our tendency to anthropomorphize, we should bear in mind that 'the Word' does not refer to 'speaking' in the way we commonly understand it.

The ancient Mayans put it similarly in the opening words of the *Popol Vuh*: "This is the account of when all is still, silent and placid. All is silent and calm. Hushed and empty is the womb of the sky. These, then, are the first words, the first speech." Many Hindus and Buddhists regard 'Aum' as "the primordial sound or Vibratory Word,"[4] and Islamic cosmology says: '*Kun fa-yakun*'—when God said 'Be', it became."[5]

Such teachings have been fundamental to the faith of billions throughout history. Even great scientific minds acknowledge the essential role of vibration in the universe. A quote attributed to Nikola Tesla claims, "If you want to find the secrets of the universe, think in terms of energy, frequency and vibration."

What is the meaning and value of these cryptic statements? How are they applicable to life beyond vague and superstitious assertions about the origins and principles of the universe? These words attempt to condense an entire cosmos of phenomena into abbreviated claims that beg many questions. Ultimately, the deepest level of understanding is that which is beyond words.

The Tao that can be told is not the eternal Tao;
The name that can be named is not the eternal name.
The Nameless is the origin of Heaven and Earth.

— *Lao Tzu (Tao Te Ching)*

If the universe is mental, from where do thoughts come and go when they enter and leave our minds? Where does suffering go when we transcend our relationship to it? Pleasure and pain are equally fleeting—impermanent—as are all sense forms: physical, emotional, or otherwise.

Physics tells us that all energy changes states, but is never created or destroyed. Perhaps there is a way to experience silence and stillness in which no sensation or thought-form is present, yet consciousness continues to function. That is a deeply personal journey, which only inner-work will reveal.

2

VIBRATION: THE BODY OF SOUND

Once the whole is divided, the parts need names.

— *Lao Tzu (Tao Te Ching)*

To fully appreciate sound, we must experience it in a broader context, beyond the constraints of limited definitions. A song belongs to the category of music, and music to the category of sound. In turn, sound falls under the umbrella of vibration. Vibration is a behavior of energy. There are visible and audible forms of vibration (among others not readily perceived by the five basic human senses). Vibration, characterized by movement, requires applied energy. We may say that energy is a fundamental raw material of the universe. A sufficient energy grid can power anything connected to it, and the cosmic energy grid appears to have an unlimited capacity.

Energy is both the fuel and substance of creation. Energy without motion is unmanifest, pure, potential creative force. It is whole, undifferentiated, static and inherently unobservable since it lacks form or behavior. When potential energy is set in motion, vibration occurs. To know what causes motion is to know the generative principle of life. Energy is channeled and divided into an infinite array of forms and forces (frequencies or vibrations). Different rates and patterns of motion produce different vibrations according to complex factors.

Light, sound and other energetic currents interact in many ways. They reflect, refract, diffuse, diffract, resonate, reverberate and coalesce to create forms. A human being is an amalgamation of vibrations, with each cell and organ operating according to its own design. Our visible bodies reflect color as light waves. Sonically we produce various frequencies as well. Beyond these two types of vibration, others are at play (sensorial, mental, emotional, hormonal, etc.).

Any serious research of sound requires an exploration of its relationship to acoustics and vibration in general. This could include visible and non-visible light spectrums, quantum mechanics, wave and particle theory, energy healing, neurology and practically any observable phenomena that interact with the senses or are detectable and measurable by other means. In a vibrational universe, everything is interacting. Less immediately apparent is how these interdisciplinary researches intersect with the world of sound, meditation, healing and music.

Science, spirituality and art are mutually influencing today's paradigms of health and consciousness. Holistic therapies rooted in ancient wisdom are finding parallels in evolving scientific perspectives on the nature of reality. The fields of medicine and psychology are amassing an enormous body of case studies proving the benefits and efficacy of vibration-based technologies. Examples include MRI's, EEG's, x-rays, sonar, ultrasound, sonograms, and various forms of sound, light or heat therapies. There is extensive literature documenting this, providing ample evidence for the scientific legitimacy of these claims (i.e. *This is Your Brain on Music, Musicophilia, The Music Instinct, Biological Rhythms in Human and Animal Physiology* and *Sound Medicine*).

Sound is not merely a physical phenomenon. It can be explored through a philosophical, spiritual, direct experiential, psychological or other scientific lens. This book is intended to highlight such intersections and focus more principally on sound *itself*, rather than its particular applications and anecdotal effects.

Question your own understanding of sound. What are your basic beliefs and assumptions about how it manifests and interacts with life?

You may perceive sound as emanating from an external source, but where and how does that sense-perception arise *within* you? From the perspective of linear time and space, an object is struck and caused to vibrate. These vibrations travel outwards in all directions from a point of origin until they hit your eardrum and trigger a response in the brain, at which point you make a complex series of interpretations about what a particular sound is, where and why it is happening.

For a moment, suspend your disbelief; move beyond cause and effect. Consider the possibility that sound arises *at the moment* you perceive it. The perceiver and the perceived are inseparably linked in a process of dependent origination (an ancient Buddhist teaching reminiscent of quantum entanglement). There is absolutely no time lag or space required for the sound to reach you from its point of origin. Rather, it is a simultaneous arising of a mental projection which manifests in so-called 'outer' reality. As Gautama Buddha teaches, "All you are arises with your thoughts. With your thoughts you make the world." Does the world determine your perception, or do you in some sense determine your world by the way you think and act? Experiments in quantum physics are just beginning to acknowledge the role of the observer in determining outcomes (consider the 'double-slit experiment', which studies wave and particle pattern formation).

As a dreamer awakens to discover they were in a dream, so too may the living come to die and realize eternal life. A vaster reality awaits us, as soon as we stop taking for granted what neither science nor religion can prove. Theories are like fragments of a broken mirror, reflecting pieces of the truth.

Art is how we decorate space.
Music is how we decorate time.

— Michel Basquiat

Dualistic distinctions between self and other, internal and external would have you believe that cause and effect govern the process, but observing with greater *presence*, one can assimilate sensations with a less divided, more integrated consciousness. Your being is inseparable from the body of the Earth, the cosmos itself and all stimuli that arise in nature. You are inseparable from the progression of time; from its principle unity, origin and dissolution. Does your past exist outside of you? You are an extension of it.

> *The distinction between past, present and future is only a stubbornly persistent illusion.*
>
> — *Albert Einstein*

You are constantly integrating vibrations from many sources. For instance, you process energy from the sun by digesting plants. Your body transforms nutrients into flesh, blood, bones and so on, which will one day be reabsorbed by the Earth. The water cycle is another example of a natural, sublime process. All matter is interconnected and changes forms (phase shifts) from one state to another. The stars and moons, planets and the air you breathe constitute your experience of yourself no less than your thoughts, feelings and physical impulses, although they may seem remote, irrelevant—even alien.

The point at which we create a barrier of separation between ourselves and the universe around us is the point at which friction or conflict can emerge. Disharmony is born from the belief that something is out of place and does not belong. Harmony is the result of unifying apparently disparate energies. These forces are recontextualized (harmonized) into beauty, perfection and wholeness, not by conquering or casting out, but by complementing, integrating and balancing. This is an internal process of reorienting one's own perception of favorable and unfavorable conditions. Resolution is not strictly dependent on external factors, but on one's relationship to them as they occur.

When we struggle against thoughts and feelings, suppressing and repressing them, rejecting ourselves and judging the process, cognitive dissonance prevents inner harmony. Eventually, all of this must be brought into alignment or the cracks will expand into treacherous ravines that are increasingly difficult to reconcile as we become more divided.

> *Now, if I do anything, it is to tune souls instead*
> *of instruments; to harmonize people instead of notes.*
> *If there is anything in my philosophy, it is the law of*
> *harmony: that one must put oneself in harmony with*
> *oneself and with others. I have found in every word*
> *a certain musical value, a melody in every thought,*
> *harmony in every feeling.*
>
> *— Hazrat Inayat Khan*
> *(The Mysticism of Music, Sound and Word)*

Every component of the universe has an identity: particular attributes which define it according to the observer. Each object holds to its center, even a vaporous cloud. Yet paradoxically, the true center of the universe is within you, at the core of what 'you' are; the wellspring of consciousness and the fountain of life itself—your innate origin. To explore these mysteries is to turn the gaze of consciousness neither outward nor inward, but both at once, beyond duality, open as a shattered vessel that is finally allowed to flow, welcoming light into shadows of the unconscious.

> *He will cultivate the harmony of his body for the sake of*
> *the consonance of his soul . . . if indeed he is to be truly*
> *trained in music and poetry.*
>
> *— Plato (Republic IX)*

Allow more expansive energies to flow through and from you, unobstructed. Where illusion and attachment to false beliefs are concerned, resistance is eventually dissolved by more stable vibrations of deeper truth. A river will merge with the ocean, does it fear losing itself through that process of expansion?

The opposite of life is not death. The opposite of death is birth. Life has no opposite. Non-existence is a figment of your imagination, an inexhaustible riddle for philosophers (lovers of wisdom, not necessarily wise people; *philo* = love, *soph* = wisdom). Just as silence is out of earshot and darkness cannot be seen, lifelessness belongs to the uncreated. Because you exist, you are created. Life is your essence. Not even death can uncreate you and all you have seen. Because it has arisen, there is a source. What could stifle that source? The universe may reserve some partition for the unborn, but if so it is already sharing space with the creative, generative principle.

We must be willing to surrender our assumptions about the nature of reality in order to remain open to illumination. Otherwise we are mere projectors. A screen is blank to receive light. It is only useful in neutrality.

Sound is received by an open ear, and an ear is only as open as the mind of the listener. One can hear without listening. One can hear without understanding. One can hear without knowledge or wisdom, just as one can speak without truth or love.

Experiencing the bidirectionality of sound places you at the center of filtering both what you give and receive. This is your art of interfacing with the world. If you hide in inner corners from yourself, weaving webs of beliefs that become so many cobwebs in your worldview, then unconsciously due to fear and ignorance, your responses are adversely conditioned by your assumptions and patterns of behavior to the point that reality is virtually indistinguishable from delusion. Thoughts cannot solve it. Logic cannot unravel it. Those are closed systems.

The universe exceeds them because it contains them, along with countless alternatives you have not imagined.

Walk a mile in another's shoes. See through the eyes of an enemy. Love a stranger. Exercise compassion. When you are compassionate with yourself, you allow yourself to be without judgment. You are the watcher, observing all experiences as they rise, fall and pass through the ever-changing present, without needing to understand, explain, evaluate or rationalize them intellectually. Distinguish between what is temporary and what is eternal; then you will contact the universal field from which sound emerges and returns like waves of the ocean.

A sound is a seed. Once planted, it develops. The growth and expansion of the seed will ultimately yield its fruit. It may sustain for generations. Even long after extinction the environment holds a memory of prior life and impact. There is no erasing the past. Somewhere in the universe all is recorded, if only in the endless reverberations of cause and effect. Cultivating new seeds may need to occur in a decaying bed of ancient vibrations. How can we work with old energies to recycle them into something relevant to the present moment?

Scientists have effectively reprogrammed DNA by signaling it with sound waves (part of emerging research in the field of epigenetics).[6] We must be prepared to transform our fear, hatred, jealousy and grief as fuel in the fire of creation, along with our so-called 'positive' qualities. Since energy is neutral in essence, there is no need to qualify things as subjectively bad or unwanted. They simply *are*. As the atom is split to release incredible force, any seed can be unlocked to reveal its innate creative and destructive potential. If you label something as an 'angry' vibration, it will be met as anger. Perpetuation, not transmutation, will occur. Your radio will be tuned to anger. Being present with anger, while directing it towards peace, is an alchemical process. How can one make gold out of lead, or strength out of cowardice? How can one transform hatred into love or fear into peace?

Awareness alone is not enough. At a certain moment, we must take the reins of energy and steer it towards a goal, with purpose and intention, even if the goal is simply 'objective presence.' Willpower is the means by which awareness, with intention, becomes action. An underdeveloped willpower inevitably flounders. It cannot sustain effort or withstand challenges.

Do not regret a seed once it is planted. Do not loathe the cards in your hand. You hold what you hold, nothing else. Now you must play according to your lot. How it came to be yours is beside the point. It is already yours—too late to reject. It belongs to no one else, and their conditions are not yours either.

In reality, everything is interconnected, participatory and complementary. Your duty as an energetic harmonizer is to apply yourself to the work of bringing peace where there is discord, sewing love where there is disrespect, sharing wisdom where there is ignorance, seeing truth beyond illusion.

> *Lord, make me an instrument of your peace.*
> *Where there is hatred, let me sow love;*
> *where there is injury, pardon;*
> *where there is doubt, faith;*
> *where there is despair, hope;*
> *where there is darkness, light;*
> *and where there is sadness, joy.*
>
> *O Divine Master, grant that I may not so much seek*
> *to be consoled as to console;*
> *to be understood as to understand;*
> *to be loved as to love.*
> *For it is in giving that we receive;*
> *it is in pardoning that we are pardoned;*
> *and it is in dying that we are born to eternal life. Amen.*
>
> — *St. Francis of Assisi*

There is nothing in the universe which is unlike something else. There is nothing in the universe which is just like something else. Not one seed in nature is without its purpose—whether to rot or flourish. Either way, it feeds the life process, however prosperous it becomes on its own, for the prosperity of the whole is shared by all. There is a balanced distribution of cosmic (some might call it karmic) justice through the law of interdependence.

A sound may be long or short, loud or soft, but its value is no greater or less because of this. Its function is its own, perfect in the way it converses with life as a whole. The listener is needed for the speaker to be heard, and the speaker is needed for the listener to receive. Both are useful and essential in their archetypal roles.

If a tree falls in the woods and no one is there to hear it, you might ask how one knew it fell at all? The impact is recorded everywhere. Come before or return after, what once was standing now is fallen. Do you need to be present during the fall to witness that a change has taken place?

Life is defined as much by what we do *not* hear as what we *do* hear. Character is determined as much by what we *do* as what we do *not*. Whether anyone bears witness to your inner process, you can rest assured of what you have experienced. No one needs to validate your faith. No scientific method can supersede your own observation from within the seat of consciousness. In that sense, the cards you hold are revealed to no one but 'God' (call it *Mystery*) within you. You are a seed. In whose hand are you held? In what soil are you planted? By what energies are you nourished?

You cannot hide your true nature forever. Even behind superficial smiles, automatic pleasantries and attempts to seek attention (whether positive or negative), a truly perceptive person sees through the mask of personality. They can feel the heart behind your words and actions and know, by witnessing your impact on the world, what kind of person you have cultivated yourself to be.

Reality as a whole is beyond time. A seed comes neither before nor after creation. It is simply part of the All. Understand your place in life; by natural law, you will know what must be done to be in harmony with primordial nature. Be diligent in tilling the soil of your spirit and wise in choosing the seed of your planting, caring in tending the life you nurture and timely in harvesting the fruit of your labor. Remember that nature belongs to no one. You are simply a caretaker.

A seed is to a tree what birth is to your life, or a note is to a melody. You are like a song. Your life has its beginning, middle and end in this world, but that which sings life through you is the eternal, fertile plane from which you spring.

3

EXPERIENCING THE UNSEEN: THE INVISIBLE EFFECTS OF SOUND

To the vibrations that are transmitted directly to our consciousness by our organs of sense we give names according to the sensations we feel: matter, sound, electricity, heat, taste, smell, light. The still higher, immaterial energies and radiations, perceptible only by means of our brain and nerve centers, we call thought waves, idea waves. Beyond them there are still higher, more penetrating rays and frequencies, all the way up to the very highest all-pervading frequencies of the divine-creative power: life itself! We can only perceive these frequencies as a state of consciousness.

— *Elisabeth Haich (Initiation)*

The exploration of sound vibration and its effects on the world requires a willingness to acknowledge the unseen. The axiom, 'to see is to believe' must be reimagined. It is obvious that 'unseen' forces have a tremendous impact on our world. Whether we're considering gravity, heat, radio waves or the inner world of thoughts and feelings, unseen vibrations not only travel through space but can impact cells, molecular structure, DNA and can influence our states of consciousness.

I often tell people before beginning a sound bath (aptly named because sound travels in waves) to consider the notion that sound vibrations penetrate the human body. When we hear a car pass by, we know that sonic vibrations penetrate solid matter, because even with windows and doors shut we hear what happens outside. The rumbling of a truck can shake the ground beneath our feet and cause a glass of water to ripple. Vibrations penetrate not only glass, wood and stone, but flesh, blood and bone as well.

We are largely composed of water, and the water circulating throughout our body is a conductor of sound. When we calm down, release tension and open ourselves deeply through muscle relaxation and reduction of mental effort, we prepare ourselves to receive the benefits of vibrational therapy more deeply. *Yoga Nidra* is a practice of conscious relaxation, and *savasana* (a yogic posture in which one lies down on one's back, completely supported by the ground) is recommended for releasing tension, promoting spinal alignment and assimilating energy.

Strong belief systems can create obstructions to experiencing the world in new ways. It is almost impossible to expand one's worldview while holding on to rigid beliefs based on elaborate (though often incorrect or incomplete) structures of supposed evidence and rationale. The placebo effect is a clear demonstration of this principle. A person's faith or belief in the efficacy of a treatment can make all the difference in its results. At a certain point, skepticism, doubt, condescension and ignorant assumptions may completely block access to healing and understanding.

None of this is to suggest that one should believe arbitrarily in unprovable pseudo-science, nor is it intended to deter critical thinking and disciplined experimentation, or to disempower reason. It is not meant to encourage blind faith, subscribe to irrelevant dogma, or develop religious or superstitious attitudes.

Dissolving barriers allows us to see beyond the narrow confines of what we assume to be true. Science and philosophy have repeatedly shown us that even long-held stances defended by highly respected individuals are consistently rendered obsolete by advances in understanding and new evidence. Even Einstein had qualms with quantum mechanics, which has proven to be a vital horizon in science. We must be willing to integrate new information as it becomes available; otherwise, we become relics.

People are often afraid of the unseen. They are afraid of the future, afraid of death, afraid of poverty, afraid of sickness, afraid of stillness and facing their inner world. Many people fear their intuitions, deep thoughts, dreams and psychic abilities. We know that communication can travel invisibly by air. We have cell phones, satellites, and computers. Do you realize that you are equipped with advanced, internal wireless technology as well?

Longtime lovers can communicate without needing to say anything. Good friends often complete each other's sentences. People sometimes wake up in the middle of the night in panic before receiving a phone call telling them a family member has passed away. There are countless documented cases of such phenomena, including studies of 'astral travel' and dreaming in which people are able to describe in detail the contents of a room they have never visited.[7] Much of human communication is non-verbal. Information is transmitted through body language, facial expressions and a range of nonverbal chemical cues (i.e. pheromones), magnetic and electric signals.

> *Signal averaging techniques are used to show that one's electrocardiogram (ECG) signal is registered in another person's electroencephalogram (EEG) and elsewhere on the other person's body. While this signal is strongest when people are in contact, it is still detectable when subjects are in proximity without contact.*
>
> *— HeartMath Institute*[8]

Just as the ocean is one interconnected body of water, the air is also a singular, undivided structure on the earth. We share one atmosphere. There is air in water and water in air. Things which appear disconnected participate in each other's existence. Photons from a star reach across millions of light-years. The illusions of separation we experience due to subject-object consciousness prevent us from acknowledging the deeper truth: we are touching the stars and they are touching us.

Cease separating yourself from the source of sound. Where does sound arise? Is a sound produced by an instrument alone? Can sound perception ever be objective? Each point in a room has a unique orientation to a given sound, with a different spatial relationship to its properties of resonance and reverberation. Or consider the Doppler effect, which describes a perceived change in the frequency of a wave as the source and the observer move toward or away from each other. Furthermore, the human ear perceives sound differently than the ear of other lifeforms. Sonic perception is subjective.

Culturally, people develop differing attitudes towards various tones, languages, sounds, themes and musical styles. We can call this 'sonic connotation' conditioned by a listener's disposition and upbringing. Every vibration is filtered and interpreted through uniquely developed cognitive lenses.

It is possible to suspend this judgemental, analytical mind; to allow sound to be without any thoughts about how it is being produced, where or why.

For a trained musician, it is especially important to transcend rational analysis in the context of sound meditation. It may *sound* like music, but it is not functioning simply as music, just as yoga may *look* like exercise but is not. Yoga is a psycho-physical practice that involves much more than the body alone, for instance willpower and emotional flexibility. Arbitrary ideas about what is beautiful, what is harmonious and what is theoretically 'correct' will only prevent a person from understanding the deeper ways in which vibrations interact.

It has been shown that when you simply *think* about performing an action, the muscles involved with that action are physically engaged, as impulses are sent to those parts of the body to prepare them. This is a way in which thoughts become things. We don't realize how tangibly our visualization powers create a reciprocal response in the world, both within and around us.

As the old adage goes: *you'll hit what you're trying to avoid by focusing on it.* Your experience of life responds to the focus of your attention. Your intentions influence your actions. Your conscious and unconscious habits impact your mentality. With this knowledge, you can begin to empower your creative mind to envision solutions, invoke forces, conduct healing and deepen interactions between vibrations on all levels.

Normally, we think of sound as an invisible force. Of course it can be rendered visible through cymatics and graphic visualizers, but sound can also activate sense impressions within us. For instance, if you hear a lion's growl, you can picture a lion in your mind without seeing it physically. This is an activation of visual perception through sound. If you hear ice breaking, you can smell the cold winter air. If you hear someone crunching, you might imagine the taste of potato chips. The vibrant dimensions of literature have the capacity to activate all of our senses. This is the power of the word, of storytelling. Our senses are interdependent, producing a composite experience. The 'invisible' world of sound can thus be interpreted through other senses. Modern medicine refers to this as synesthesia.

In reality there is one sense. It is that sense which, through these five different organs, experiences life and distinguishes life in five different forms. And so all that is audible and all that is visible is one and the same.

— *Hazrat Inayat Khan*
(The Spiritual Significance of Color and Sound)

As the enormity of an iceberg is concealed underwater, the volume of sonic information behind what we hear remains largely 'unheard'. The physical force and audible impression of the sound are real, but they only tell part of the story. One does not hear with ears alone. In conjunction with the entire body, a full spectrum of sonic data is detected and interpreted down to the cellular and molecular level. Beyond physicality, abstract properties of sound with regards to emotion, intention and philosophy are also transmitted.

> *Believe nothing you hear, and only one half that you see.*
> — *Edgar Allen Poe*

Intuition tells you when someone rubs you the wrong way. You can read when a person is lying to you. Empathy allows you to feel what someone else is going through. No words are necessary. The proverbial elephant in the room is telling you: *it goes without saying.*

4

EVERYTHING IS VIBRATION: THE RELATIONSHIP BETWEEN SOUND AND LIGHT

Energy moves in Waves. Waves move in patterns. Patterns move in rhythms. A human being is just that—energy, waves, patterns, rhythms. Nothing more. Nothing less. A dance.

— *Gabrielle Roth, 5Rhythmns Founder*

A good friend once told me to explore how the fractals of light relate to the fractals of sound. He suggested that I close my eyes, play a chord on the guitar and observe what geometries or images come to mind. At the time, I had no idea what he meant. The properties of light and sound seemed disconnected to me. Years later, I am finding more connections.

Fractals are essentially infinite, self-repeating structures that can teach us a great deal about the nature of holograms, the universe and the logic of mathematics. Like other areas of what is commonly labeled 'sacred geometry,' fractals reveal the infinite creative potential of the universe and illuminate the interconnectedness of all phenomena. Snowflakes, conch shells, spiral galaxies, coiled DNA and plant life clearly illustrate the principle of fractals at play in nature. Structures such as these closely adhere to the Golden Ratio (Phi) or Fibonacci Sequence, revealing a mathematical logic inherent to nature's creative expression.

Note the repeating patterns in these images from nature:

One day I visited the Tibet Arts and Healing center in Salem, Massachusetts, and spoke with a good friend who shared many things with me about Tibetan mantra and Himalayan instruments.

"Look," he told me, "this singing bowl makes a six-pointed star when you fill it with water and play it." He held the bowl in the open palm of his hand, half-filled with water, and started circling a felt-wrapped mallet around the rim until a six-pointed star appeared, spinning on the surface of the water. I was amazed, because the six-pointed star (also associated with the Star of David in the Jewish tradition and the *Merkavah* in Kabbalah), often associated with the heart chakra (*Anahata* in Sanskrit) was inscribed into the bowl itself:

I was observing a simple and practical demonstration of cymatics, a realm of science that explores vibratory phenomena using various resonating diaphragms (membranes) and mediums including water, sand, gas, flame and other particle fields to render sound waves visible.[9] Cymatics experiments have shown that certain frequencies produce specific, repeatable geometric patterns and behaviors of motion.[10]

The power of sound waves to alter physical objects goes far beyond cymatics. The controversial work of Masaru Emoto and his experiments programming water molecules with meditation and mantra suggest that mental and spoken vibrations could affect the properties of crystalline structures. Furthermore, researchers in the field of acoustophoresis (literally 'sound migration') have successfully levitated small objects using an acoustic field, proving that sound has the capacity to physically displace objects.[11]

Sound and light are emitted by all vibrating objects. Since vibration produces heat and heat is measured on the electromagnetic (light) spectrum, we can say that anything which vibrates is measurable in terms of frequency. Vibration also produces mechanical pressure waves (sound) when particles are pushed against neighboring particles.[12] Since 'non-visible' sound waves can be used to move visible objects, it is clear that sound and light act upon each other. Understanding this interdependence has many potential applications, including the targeted distribution of medicines within the body.

All of this is relevant to sound healing because we are learning that sound can produce harmonic structures, geometrically balanced shapes and wave patterns that may be more or less harmonious with the human body and its surrounding environment. They can even disrupt physical blockages. The capacity to manipulate harmonic shapes and speeds of rotation has great use when it comes to unblocking energetic channels in the meridians, improving circulation and encouraging target brainwave states (delta, theta, alpha, beta, gamma) as well as stimulating electrical activity in the body and promoting coherence between respiration, heart rate and blood pressure.[13]

It has already been theorized and tested that sick (improperly functioning) cells are vibrating in a way that is out of harmony with health and balance. Exposing such cells to regular vibratory levels can optimize the healing process. The controversial work of Royal Raymond Rife and his Rife Machine is one example of applying these principles to healing technology.[14]

Tom Kenyon has conducted pioneering research in the field of psychoacoustics for decades, and his work reveals that prolonged exposure to certain frequencies can entrain the brain and promote healthy sleep and relaxation, with other beneficial results.[15] Hypnosis and ASMR (autonomous sensory meridian response) are related fields that implement the essence of this research. Again, there is ample literature on all of these subjects available elsewhere for those interested in verifying the scientific legitimacy of these claims.

Understanding that sound can induce physical and emotional response is key to realizing that on some level, thoughts make things. The words we choose have an impact on our world and the inner dialogue we have about life. Gautama Buddha expressed this concisely, thousands of years ago, in the Dhammapada—valuable information for practitioners of sound meditation:

> *We are what we think.*
> *All that we are arises with our thoughts.*
> *With our thoughts we make the world.*
> *Speak or act with an impure mind*
> *And trouble will follow you*
> *As the wheel follows the ox that draws the cart.*
> *We are what we think.*
> *All that we are arises with our thoughts.*
> *With our thoughts we make the world.*
> *Speak or act with a pure mind*
> *And happiness will follow you*
> *As your shadow, unshakable.*

— *Gautama Buddha (The Dhammapada: Choices)*

As I've continued meditating on my friend's suggestion to visualize the fractal relationship of light to sound, I've become increasingly aware of the power of the Word. The role of sound in the process of creation must be explored for any serious practitioner to realize the many ways in which thoughts, words and sounds affect oneself and others. Willpower, vision, determination, creativity, inspiration, organization—all of these influence action.

In turn, the external world reflects our meditation—at times inspiring, at times overwhelming. The relationship goes both ways. Different environments affect one's state of consciousness, much in the way that properties of acoustic spaces impact the quality of sound experienced within and around them. The shapes of instruments, architectural designs of concert halls and theaters, and the substances used in their construction alter the resonance, volume, tonal quality and reverberation of sounds produced within them. Likewise, other vibrational properties such as the presence of natural light, plant life and paint colors have an impact on the psyche. A dirty, dismal space may be less conducive for people to meditate or work in than a clean, well-organized environment. Musicians often report feeling inspired or uninspired by various concert settings and audience energies, and the need to 'tune' the room and audience to the experience before playing.

The outer environment reflects the inner and vice versa. The principles of fractals and the holographic theory of the universe encourage us to examine the cross-relationships between seemingly disconnected elements. Light and sound are two such elements which, upon closer examination, are interdependent.

5

FREQUENCY: PATTERNS OF IDENTITY

A keen observation shows that the whole universe is a single mechanism working by the law of rhythm; the rise and fall of the waves, the ebb and flow of the tide, the waxing and waning of the moon, the sunrise and the sunset, the change of the seasons, the moving of the earth and of the planets, the whole cosmic system and the constitution of the entire universe are working under the law of rhythm. Cycles of rhythm, with major and minor cycles.

— *Hazrat Inayat Khan*
(The Mysticism of Music, Sound and Word)

The world we perceive is a tapestry of light and sound vibrations. We observe these luminous and sonic structures when their waveforms reach our organs of perception at specific, dependable rates. Frequency refers to a periodic cycle. It implies symmetry, consistency—recalling a prior state at regular intervals.

When someone goes to the same restaurant often, we say that they 'frequent' the place, or that they are a 'regular.' Regulating means 'to control or maintain the rate or speed' at which something operates.

Sound frequency is measured in hertz (Hz). The volume, or loudness of a sound is measured in amplitude (vertical) and its speed (oscillations per second) in wavelength (horizontal). Amplitude is quantified in decibels (dB's). This is graphed as a sine wave in two dimensions:

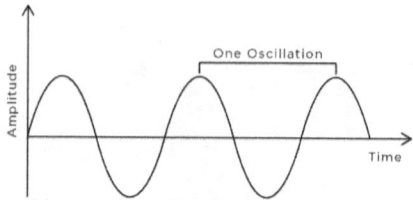

Where there are particles to vibrate, sound can travel. Since vibration is characterized by motion, the peaks and valleys of sine waves relate to high and low pressure (compression and rarefaction) where particles are closer together or farther apart, respectively.

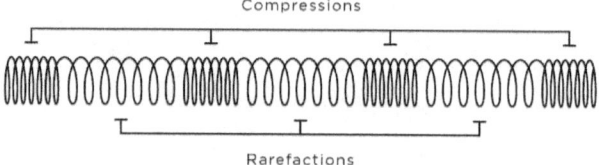

Sound travels through air, but it can also travel through water and denser substances like metal or wood. The denser the substance, the faster sound can travel, since particles are packed more closely together, making it easier for waves to transfer between them. The speed of sound in air is around 760 mph (343 m/s), but sound travels roughly five times faster through water and 15 times faster through iron than it does through air.[16] The speed and distance a sound can travel are affected by temperature, pressure, density and humidity (among other factors), since these affect particle behavior and therefore the waves that pass through them.

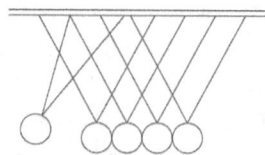

Newton's Cradle expresses how energy is transferred
through particles in a mechanical pressure wave.

Environmental variables produce some interesting sonic phenomena. The National Oceanic and Atmospheric Administration describes how whales make use of 'sound channels' to communicate across vast distances: "The thermocline is a region characterized by rapid change in temperature and pressure which occurs at different depths around the world . . . The area in the ocean where sound waves refract up and down is known as the 'sound channel.' The channeling of sound waves allows sound to travel thousands of miles without the signal losing considerable energy."[17]

The distance a sound can travel depends on the amount of energy used to produce it and how long it takes for that energy to dissipate in the environment. Some energy is converted into heat, released through particle collisions as sound waves interact with objects. These interactions can manifest in several ways:

Absorption: energy from a sound wave is transferred (transduced) into the material it passes through.

Cancellation: two or more opposing waves reduce or negate each other.

Diffraction: a wave passes around an object of similar or smaller size to its wavelength.

Diffusion: scattering waves through space so that they don't cross the same paths on which they arrived.

Interference: two or more waves can interact in various ways.

> 1. Constructive interference: the sum of two waves increases the amplitude.

> 2. Destructive interference: the sum of two waves decreases the amplitude.

3. Standing wave: the same wave travels
back over itself.

Reflection: a wave bounces off an object and returns
to its point of origin.

Refraction: a wave bounces off an object and
changes direction.

Resonance: a wave matches the natural frequency
of a space, creating standing waves.

As a sound decays, its intensity and volume decrease over
time. One of the loudest sounds ever recorded was a volcanic
eruption in 1883 that reportedly produced "a blast of high
pressure air so powerful that it ruptured the eardrums of sailors
40 miles away" and "continued to sweep onward, reverberating
for days across the globe. The atmosphere was ringing like a
bell, imperceptible to us but detectable by our instruments."[18]

Beyond Earth's atmospheric conditions, scientists say that
sound waves cannot travel in the vacuum of space since there
are no particles to vibrate. However, the astral bodies themselves
can be seen as countless particles vibrating on a galactic scale,
so perhaps there are cosmic waves beyond normal human
perception, producing sounds of tremendous wavelengths. This
may be the notion of primordial sound—the sound of creation
which permeates the universe—which the Hindus call 'Aum'
and Judeo-Christians call 'the Word'.

At any rate, most sound frequencies are imperceptible to us.
440 hertz refers to the number of cycles per second required for
our ears to detect a pitch we call 'A' in standard tuning. Higher
and lower frequencies (faster and slower vibrations) result in
different pitches. The following diagram represents the note A
at 440 Hz and the same pitch (A) one octave higher, where

its speed doubles to A880 Hz (ratio 2:1). The sine wave is an essential geometry of sound.

SOUND WAVES

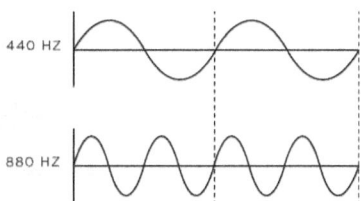

440 HZ

880 HZ

Principle of the octave:
A lower pitch has a longer wavelength. This is because it vibrates more slowly, which means it takes longer to return to the starting point of the cycle. An octave refers to a frequency that is in a 2:1 ratio to another frequency.

An in-depth exploration of how hearing works from a physiological perspective can be found elsewhere, but here it is worth noting that the human ear can detect sounds within a typical maximum range of 20 to 20,000 hertz. Of course, sound waves can be much higher (faster and shorter) and lower (slower and longer) than this, but they are generally not recognized by human ears, although they can be felt in other ways.

Similarly, the visible and non-visible light spectrum is measured and divided into ranges of nanometers. However, light itself is composed of particles (photons) whereas sound requires a particle field to vibrate. Light below the visible spectrum is called infrared, and light above the visible spectrum is called ultraviolet. Sound below the audible spectrum is called infrasonic, and sound above the audible spectrum is called ultrasonic.

Light Waves

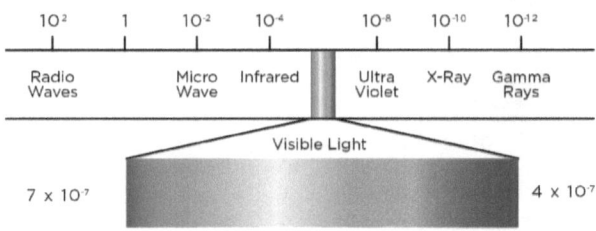

Like sound waves, light waves are divided into a range of frequencies. Some are visible to the human eye, some are not.

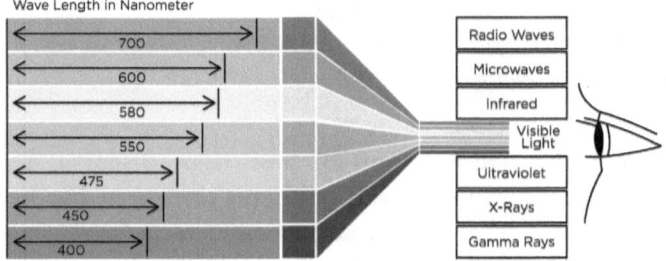

Different colors of light travel at different speeds, or wavelengths.

The study of the creation of the universe is fundamentally an examination of how nothing came to be something. In other words, it attempts to explain how vibrations arose from stillness. From that perspective, we may consider that stillness began to 'speed up.' Therefore, slower vibrations would first reach the audible spectrum, since visible light frequencies move 'faster' than sound (a car must go 30 mph before it can reach 60 mph). Perhaps for this reason, creation stories often refer to sound as manifesting *before* light. Of course, sound and light are not interchangeable in physics, as we are dealing with mechanical and electromagnetic waves respectively. Nevertheless, it is worth considering if the big bang implies 'turning on and speeding up.' This would imply that infrasonic and infrared structures came into existence *before* ultrasonic and ultraviolet frequencies. Likewise, the ultimate fate of our universe may depend on the tendency of these vibrations to eventually slow down and return to stillness. In the context of meditation, stilling and quieting the mind is a practice of slowing down and bringing an end to the arising of thoughtforms.

If sound and light waves do not maintain their rates of speed, the sense objects we perceive become unstable. A musical note goes out of tune (sharp or flat). A light bulb dims, brightens or shatters with excess current. In the extreme, our world would be rendered incomprehensible (chaotic) if the frequencies we are accustomed to strayed from their vibrational structures. Identity depends on stability. Everything from a plant to a planet is composed of dependable, interrelated vibrations that compose the object. Like an onion built in layers, or a tapestry woven from many strands, a multitude of vibrations participate in the creation of an object. Every cell vibrates. Every organ vibrates. Every voice vibrates.

Consider the frequencies of the Earth itself, known as Schumann resonances, or the 'Music of the Spheres' produced by the friction of planetary orbits. The Schumann Resonance refers to an electromagnetic frequency that resonates between the Earth's surface and the ionosphere. These two geophysical boundaries act as a 'waveguide' for the resonance produced by photons (sustained by lightning) which become trapped in the atmosphere. The fundamental wavelength of the Schumann Resonance is equal to the circumference of the Earth, and is sometimes considered to be the 'heartbeat of the earth'. The 'Music of the Spheres' refers to a Pythagorean concept in which the patterns of planetary bodies produce choreographed movements, reminiscent of song and dance. In modern times, science has confirmed that even planets themselves produce frequencies which can be interpreted as audible sound through human implements.[19]

There are as many voices as there are souls;
they cannot be classified.

— Hazrat Inayat Khan
(The Effect of Sound on the Physical Body)

Stable frequency is the ground we stand on, so to speak. When a person behaves in an unexpected manner, we call their behavior 'erratic.' Entropy and chaos are frequency disruptors. 'Disruptive' frequencies *can* be beneficial (such as changing bad habits), but in general we depend on consistency to reliably process information about our reality.

This is obvious when we consider how cycles of the sun, moon and stars regulate our lives. We count on sunrise and sunset to navigate time the way we do. The seasons reliably produce weather patterns for planting, growing and harvesting. Waves of the ocean rise and fall (oscillate) with lunar cycles. As we travel the earth, sea and sky, we orient ourselves by the stars. The relatively steady force of gravity keeps us grounded to the earth.

Out of the multitude of our sense experiences we take,
mentally and arbitrarily, certain repeatedly occurring
complexes of sense impression (partly in conjunction
with sense impressions which are interpreted as signs for
sense experiences of others) and we attribute to them a
meaning—the meaning of the bodily object.

— Albert Einstein

Internally, we also depend on patterns of frequency: from the heartbeat and circulatory system, to respiration and muscle coordination.[20] Waking and sleeping, speaking and listening, motion and stasis, light and dark—these dualistic polarities can be seen as peaks and valleys (pendulum swings) in the frequencies of our lives.

We measure time itself using various types of clocks. Today, the most accurate clocks use quartz to measure frequency.[21] Countless modern technologies rely on crystals (phones, computers, etc.). Silicon valley gets its name from silicon dioxide, a chemical derived from quartz. Even atomic clocks used by Nasa rely on it, and are accurate to within one second over 10 million years.[22] Quartz is able to convert mechanical pressure into electrical energy and vice versa (piezoelectricity). The stable, hexagonal molecular structure of quartz, as well as its resultant durability, are primary factors in its usefulness. Size and shape determine its vibrational frequency, thus it can be adapted for many uses. For example, in wristwatches, quartz pieces are cut to vibrate at 32,768 Hz, a frequency divisible into the standard unit of measurement we call one second. Quartz can also store information in a form of memory. Scientists have built a quartz coin that can store 360 TB of data for billions of years.[23] Thus quartz has proven to be vital for both sound and light technology.

Interestingly, within our own bodies, crystalline structures are present in the pineal gland,[24] which helps regulate the endocrine system, hormones and bodily functions ranging from sleeping and dreaming to emotional processing and digestion.[25] For those interested in the esoteric aspects of crystal technology, parallels in modern science should illuminate their profound significance to humanity. Crystals serve as intermediaries between mechanical and electromagnetic energy; in other words: converting, amplifying (increasing) and attenuating (reducing) sound and light vibrations.

Just as there are sound and light waves that exist undetected by our eyes and ears, there are many types of vibrations in the universe which evade human perception and understanding. It requires the development of sensitive technology (both inner and outer) to observe them. To transmit and receive television and radio frequencies, we must align our instruments with particular bandwidths. If we don't like what we see or hear, we can turn it off or change the channel. Similar principles apply to consciousness.

Some say human beings are creatures of habit. Another way of putting it is to say that we are accustomed to patterns (routines of thought and behavior which we reinforce continually). This can occur on a daily basis or through other cycles of repetition. We also align with patterns in nature, such as circadian rhythms (from Latin '*circa diem*' meaning 'about a day') and menstrual cycles ('*mensis*' means month in Latin).

Habits can be psychological, emotional, physical and addictive in 'nature. This relates to frequency in the sense that habits result from cycles of repeated action. Behavioral *entrainment* reinforces predictable responses—conditioned reactions that can be difficult to deviate from. This is due to the energetic magnetism or 'gravitational' pull of habitual behavior. There are various ways to disrupt and reprogram an ingrained pattern. To do so requires forging new pathways. Abstaining from habitual action implies that *other* actions must necessarily fill the space-time in one's life that becomes available in their absence. By tuning and aligning to different frequencies, new connections are established. Modern science speaks of this in terms of neuroplasticity.

Doing the unexpected (the road less traveled) introduces an element of change that recontextualizes one's experience by presenting new information to process and integrate. The same is true of thoughtforms. If one frequently says, "I am depressed," a new intentional thought to rewrite this inner negative belief could be, "I am recovering from depression," or, "I occasionally experience symptoms of depression."[26] This allows a person to distance themselves from directly identifying *as* depressed. The person may eventually come to say, sincerely, "I am not depressed."

Of course, depression takes many forms that stem from complex factors. In many cases, a person can only overcome depression through a concerted effort to rewire neural pathways.

This can be done by cultivating physical practices (diet and exercise), meditative disciplines and emotional training such as non-violent communication, psychological healing, etc. All of these reinforce new patterns of living, which are most effective when practiced *frequently*, until they are anchored in lifestyle as healthy habits.

The *frequency* with which you practice (time of day, duration, location, specific structure of the practice, etc.) reinforces its presence and efficacy in your life. Inconsistency prolongs the transition period and weakens the magnetism of these methods. Committing to a practice routine allows one to observe growth over time. The scientific method uses controls and variables to measure results. Likewise, inner-engineering is a developmental science that employs structured methods to observe the results of psycho-physical experiments and spiritual practices.

Adhering only to one's personal comfort zone could be another type of addiction. Fear, laziness and ignorance can result in apathy and complacency. This produces a narrow bandwidth or limited worldview.

In music, we develop habits based on what we have practiced. Our ears grow accustomed to certain musical gestures, and our creativity is generally limited to the influences we have been exposed to. Once we recognize habitual rhythms, melodies and progressions, we can intentionally alter them, consciously explore new territory and attempt to work in less familiar ways. There are many compositional methods, forms and strategies. Adopting a new process, even temporarily for the sake of variety, can shake up stagnant energy and loosen the stranglehold of rote methodology.

Memory is deeply tied to music. Culturally speaking, there are national anthems, lullabies and traditional songs that live in the collective aesthetic of a social group (whether national, religious, etc.). For many people, such songs are nostalgic sources of pride, reinforced in part by countless repetitions over many decades or even centuries of dissemination.

Popular music, including classical melodies from composers like Bach, Mozart and Beethoven also function in this way, although they transcend national borders and speak more broadly to humanity. Like World Heritage Sites, UNESCO refers to such artistic contributions as, 'Intangible Cultural Heritage,' differing in that they exist as abstract forms of expression rather than concrete material objects. These cultural treasures from the art world are as important to preserve as any architectural structure.

Individually, we each have personal anthems, so to speak; songs which touch us deeply, although they may be obscure or entirely unknown to others. Such songs form close bonds with our emotions, especially when they accompany emotionally charged experiences like a marriage, funeral, separation or protest. Like a familiar smell, a song may transport us back to a time and place within our memory where love or disdain for that music was first activated.

This is partly why music therapy is so beneficial for people suffering from Alzheimer's and age-related dementia. Since music stimulates a great deal of brain activity, including memory processing, linguistic skills and emotional processing, playing music that is familiar can vividly reactivate memories and induce flashbacks.

Many of us return to songs throughout our lives. We recall words of wisdom that reassure us—perhaps the guidance of a parent, friend, book or influential teacher. These bits of life advice serve as personal proverbs or mantras and become anchored within us like a favorite song. We frequently call upon these anecdotes until they become as integral to our identity as any of our physical aspects.

6

REINCARNATION AND THE ETERNAL SOUL: CYCLES OF REBIRTH

Image courtesy of the Bhaktivedanta Book Trust International Inc.

And whoever, at the time of death, quits his body, remembering Me alone, at once attains My nature. Of this there is no doubt. Whatever state of being one remembers when he quits his body, that state he will attain without fail.

— *Bhagavad Gita: Attaining the Supreme*

Time undivided, we call eternal. Time divided, we call infinite. Time can be divided infinitely into larger or smaller segments. Many traditions speak of the eternal soul, or something akin to it by another name. For agnostics, atheists or materialists, the word 'soul' might trigger an immediate rejection. However, the concept of the soul need not be associated with religion, mere philosophy, fantasy or pseudo-science. We are treading abstract ground where words inevitably fall short of describing what is essentially the 'life-force' of a living being.

A human being has a physical body, including an energetic aura composed of heat waves, electric signals, chemical trails and so on.

One also experiences what may be called an 'emotional body.' Physical (i.e. hormonal and neurological) properties of the body affect this system, but more complex processes are also involved: personal memories, genetic factors and social conditioning that can program emotional response.

The 'mental body' may be considered a realm of pure thoughtform: imagination, ideas, intellect, rationality, etc. This part of one's self is responsible for abstract thought.

The 'astral body' experiences dreams and visions (among other sensations). In a dream one has a body that differs from the physical body. The 'dream body' can be lucidly controlled; it is in some sense *more* capable than the physical body, since its capacities are limited only by imagination. In a dream one can fly, manifest objects at will and perform feats that are considered impossible in 'waking life.' Thoughts and emotions are also present in dreams. Can you remember a dream in which you experienced visceral emotional or physical sensations? Dream states can even carry over into waking life, such as when a person awakens from a nightmare, still gripped by fear.

These definitions vary by tradition, and the delineations between physical, mental, emotional and astral or 'spiritual' bodies are somewhat arbitrary. Although we are made up of various parts (nerves, organs, bones, etc.) we are also whole, undivided lifeforms. Of the divisions between the spiritual and material planes, the Bible teaches:

There is a natural body and there is a spiritual body.

— *1 Corinthians, 15:44 (KJV)*

Render therefore unto Caesar the things which are Caesar's; and unto God the things that are God's.

— *Matthew 22:21*

Or, if you prefer, in the words of Radiohead: *"Everything in its right place."*

When a car comes into production, it is envisioned as a design concept *before* a prototype is built. Likewise, human beings must be *conceived*. Although conception may be unintentional, a human being is the result of prior actions, thoughts and feelings. There is an ongoing debate regarding when life begins. Some argue from a physical perspective, attempting to pinpoint at what stage a zygote or fetus' development constitutes 'life.' It is a question of when consciousness enters the body.

However, it could be said that life begins in the visions of a mother and father who prepare their hearts and minds for parenting. With intention (long before the birth of a child) they are already cultivating who a child is within themselves, and the environment that will welcome them. Many parents report having dreams and premonitions of their children long before pregnancy, sometimes years in advance. They may accurately anticipate gender, hair and eye color or other aspects of the child. Whether this is a lucky guess or a self-fulfilling prophecy is another matter, but the phenomenon occurs too frequently to disregard.

Kahlil Gibran speaks eloquently of a parent's journey in this excerpt from his poem "*On Children*":

> *Your children are not your children.*
> *They are the sons and daughters of Life's longing for itself.*
> *They come through you but not from you,*
> *And though they are with you yet they belong not to you.*
> *You may give them your love but not your thoughts,*
> *For they have their own thoughts.*
> *You may house their bodies but not their souls,*
> *For their souls dwell in the house of tomorrow,*
> *which you cannot visit, not even in your dreams.*

It is an unproven assumption that consciousness does not exist until it is produced by a physical body.[27] The body itself is produced within a much vaster body: the planetary body, the solar system and the universe itself. This immeasurably complex ecosystem sustains all necessary conditions to facilitate life and consciousness. Even our tiny speck of a planet hosts trillions of lifeforms.

Forms vary, but the essence remains the same. The essence of life is consciousness. This clearly takes precedence over the body itself. What use is a body without consciousness? Yet consciousness does not depend on a particular body. You can lose a limb, even your heart can be transplanted, yet it is impossible to remove consciousness from your body or you would be dead. Even people in comas and vegetative states can exhibit responses to their environment. Removing life-support systems is controversial since we don't know the inner cognitive state of a person and cannot be certain they are dead in that sense.

Consciousness is like computer software, while the body is hardware on which it runs. A computer can die but the same program could be downloaded and installed on other machines to reproduce countless sounds and images. Consciousness is an operating system of the universe (albeit vastly more complex than our primitive computer software). We are *applications of consciousness* connected to a universal web. Each of us executes personalized functions. Our lives play out like endless, unrepeatable snowflakes but the archetypes we experience are universal: birth, death, love, fear, joy, playfulness, etc.

> *Our basic emotional repertoire is shared*
> *across all human cultures.*
>
> — *(The Alexander Technique:*
> *Freedom in Thought and Action)*

It is naive to assume that the physical world gives rise to consciousness, but that consciousness cannot produce an effect on the physical world—since an abstract idea or inspiration *precedes* its physical result:

ABSTRACT/MENTAL		PHYSICAL
Inspiration	—>	Expression
Instinct	—>	Action (here the physical and mental/emotional are very close)
Idea	—>	Invention/Production
Plan	—>	Execution

The Sufi mystic Hazrat Inayat Khan taught that when spirit becomes dense, it transforms into matter, and when matter becomes rarefied, it returns to spirit. Like the water cycle, this sublime process is endless. Many traditions assert that the soul is eternal and transcends the life of the physical body. A body is to the soul what a song is to music. When silence follows a song, does music cease to exist? Likewise death does not require life to end. Rather, there is a transition from life to life, from song to song. Some call this reincarnation, science calls it the law of conservation of energy—agreeing that nothing is lost, but changes form.

Sound is an ocean in which many waves rise and fall. The universal principles of sound exist in every song, as distinct as they may appear on the surface. A song passes through time with a beginning, middle and end. It is therefore impermanent, like the body. The principle of music however, carries on, just as life carries on after someone dies. Their consciousness may dissipate, or it may remain intact even after the physical body is discarded. Do not assume either to be true. Consider it a subject of meditation, which is a scientific method of observing consciousness.

Over time, the cycle of birth and death can be seen as a frequency pattern. Each time someone dies, there is a powerful dissociation from what we call the 'human experience.' From the medical perspective, studies reveal that at the moment of death, chemicals regulated by the endocrine system flood the body. Combined with oxygen deprivation to the brain, this produces what might be considered 'hallucinatory' or 'euphoric' states. Depending on the conditions of death, these could be horrific states of fear (like having a 'bad trip'). This extreme state of altered consciousness, aided by endorphins, facilitates a depersonalized experience of one's self, whereby a merger with 'the infinite' becomes more accessible. Therapy with entheogens can have a significant, healing impact on people with trauma, fear of death, depression, addiction and a wide range of other restrictive emotional and psychological challenges. Powerful entheogenic plants enable a person to experience what some call an 'ego death,' thereby preparing us to come to terms with 'physical' death. Many people report visions of complex geometries and fractals which reveal, through light, the interconnectedness of natural structures, further deemphasizing feelings of separation.

It is worth noting that traditional healing and meditation practices with master plants (considered to be allies, teachers and spirits) incorporate many forms of vibrational therapies simultaneously. Examples of vibrational therapies include:

> SOUND: auditory medicines can involve
> chanting, instrumental music, spoken word,
> nature sounds, intentional silence, etc.

> SMELL: olfactory therapies include herbs,
> flowers, incense, perfumes and oils,
> environmental smells (forest, sea, desert, etc.)

> TOUCH: tactile therapies make use of physical
> contact, blessing and smudging with sacred
> feathers, physical postures and exercises, etc.

> SIGHT: visual therapy may involve elaborate
> altars, candles, symbolic art, guided
> visualizations, environmental scenery, etc.

> TASTE: ingested substances (food, bitter herbs,
> etc.), and abstinence from ingested substances,
> appeal to the sense of taste.

Furthermore, shamanic healing techniques make use of elemental vibrations such as heat, cold, weight and gravity, wind (e.g. breath), water, earth, and fire. All of these complex vibrational elements are balanced with intention and intuition, to guide a person through the sensitive terrain of 'ego death,' in which undesirable psychological states are confronted, integrated and ultimately transcended. Emerging from such an experience, freed from burdensome obsessions and limiting worldviews, a person is said to be 'reborn.' Thus it is perhaps more accurate to call it 'transformation' than 'death.'

In any case, the focus of one's consciousness at the moment of death is a factor in how one experiences the transition. A lifetime of behaviors and vibrational imprints such as memory, desire, attachment and regret resurface with magnified power. Any unresolved conflict in the psyche may distract the mind from equanimity, preventing it from returning to its transcendental source in the form of pure soul. It is important not to associate the soul in this context with another level of the 'self.' The soul is not an intellectual idea to be understood philosophically and cannot be compared to a human form either in substance or in its relationship to time. In general, human lives are perceived in a linear trajectory from birth to death, while the life of a soul is not strictly linear. In brief, I use the word soul to signify the total vibratory, multi-dimensional sum of one's life force. To suggest that it has a 'separate identity' is misleading.

Overidentification with the body, with other people, with shame and internal conflicts can cause cognitive dissonance (separation) and prevent complete merger with what the Bhagavad Gita refers to as "the Supreme Personality of Godhead" (the fundamental source and origin of life). Inability or refusal to achieve this merger may necessitate reincarnation. The show must go on. There is more to resolve, more to harmonize. Those ripples in the pond where the stone once fell have yet to return to calm.

After attaining Me, the great souls, who are yogis in devotion, never return to this temporary world, which is full of miseries, because they have attained the highest perfection.

— *Bhagavad Gita: Attaining the Supreme*

This is why understanding and mastering the principle of vibration is essential to every conscious being: any patterned belief we hold is a potential trap in a world of illusion. Attachment to illusion is ignorance, and ignorance causes suffering when we live according to false views that contradict eternal, natural law. An illusion is a projection, like a mirage in the desert, creating unachievable goals to try and satisfy insatiable desire. We are accustomed to wanting what we do not have, and having what we do not want . . . attachment and aversion: a vicious polarity.

You only lose what you cling to.

— *Gautama Buddha*

Since all forms rise and fall, we must accept that the body is eventually discarded. What makes the life cycle of a body any different from the life cycle of a thought or feeling? As a string is plucked to produce the sound which swells and fades— from silence to silence—we ourselves are waveforms. Our lives express periodicity.

One of the reasons why Hindus pray to Krishna, why Buddhist monks chant 'Aum', why Muslims pray five times a day towards Mecca, why Jews daven and Catholics confess—is to clear the mind of negativity and open to the divine. A lifetime of harmonizing with and patterning oneself in spirituality is believed to be preparation for the moment of death. Some call it judgment, but what happens is you judge yourself. If you harbor shame, guilt and regret, you will punish yourself in death just as you do in life. But if you cultivate peace, love, gratitude and trust, you will reward yourself in death as you do in life.

Creativity and imagination always manifest the reflection of one's focus. An artist's work reflects their meditation. A dream reflects the content of one's psyche. Like a fractal, hologram, seed or strand of DNA, humanity is made in the image and likeness of (for lack of a less conditioned word) God. That is our potential, if not our practice. Cultivating spirituality is not merely preparation for death—it is fulfillment of life. When you nourish something, it grows. When you starve it, it dies. We must breathe life into a flute or song. A string must be plucked. Music must be kept alive, with effort and intention. If not: silence. Kabbalah teaches it was not God who banished humanity from the Garden of Eden, but rather, humanity who banished God from themselves.

A person may believe in an afterlife, in reincarnation, or not. For those who hold that creation is eternal, they may consider their soul to be eternal as well. From that perspective, birth and death are doorways on the journey of the soul. This belief leads many to seek spiritual understanding. However, false constructs can develop in that process, causing a person to lead a deluded life. One must look carefully at their personal cosmology—based on science, religion or otherwise—and determine if it is compatible with reality or not. Meditation on stillness, silence and the breath can help achieve this.

The word spirit itself means 'breath', related to words like respiration. Breath gives life, but breathing is often performed unconsciously. The compulsion of life pumps our lungs like a bellows. But we can choose to meditate and practice conscious breathing, bringing awareness and control to an otherwise automatic life function. Modulating the life-force through *pranayama*, allows us to intentionally direct the flow of energy through our bodies and minds.[28] This can promote healing and regeneration throughout the psycho-physical system (cells, tissues, emotions, mental patterns, etc.). Intentional breath used in song, prayer or mantra is a key aspect of sound healing. Therefore, understanding the relationship between the breath and the human voice is vital.

Healing means to restore balance. Meditation promotes balance.[29] The root of the word meditation in Latin is *'medi'* which means 'middle.' Meditation is a common translation of the Sanskrit word *dhyana*, which has its roots in *dhi* (mind) and *yana* (moving).[30] From this definition, we can see that meditation implies working with the movement, or vibration, of the mind. Through meditation we can observe, reflect, and respond to our environment with greater awareness.

Where there is light in the soul,
there is beauty in the person.
Where there is beauty in the person,
there is harmony in the home.
Where there is harmony in the home,
there is honor in the nation.
Where there is honor in the nation,
there is peace in the world.

— *Chinese Proverb*

Gautama Buddha taught the Middle Way as a path to illumination. It is crucial to restore balance in oneself in order to help others. This is the medicine of harmony. Ultimately, the principle of harmony extends from within oneself to all life throughout the universe, where countless beings are born and die. By distinguishing that which is ephemeral from that which is eternal, we free ourselves from many limited beliefs. Some say we free ourselves from the cycle of birth and death itself.

7

HARMONY

Since sound and light are vibratory,
words, thoughts and actions resonate.
For this, a resonating body is needed.

Consciousness is like a string
ready to be plucked.
Will is the act of striking it.

Awareness is listening
and the universe is an echo chamber.

Positive and negative are matters of perspective.

You and I generate harmony,
but the song is of the Spirit.

Harmony implies division. When the whole is one, there is
nothing to harmonize. The perception of separation requires
two or more things to be harmonized. Duality is a basic division:
birth and death, self and other, friend and enemy, prosecution
and defense. Each of us, insofar as we perceive ourselves to
possess a separate identity, must learn the art of reconciliation.
To reconcile means 'to bring together again.'

There are internal and external forms of separation.

Internally, people divide themselves into body, heart, mind, spirit and so on. These various aspects of 'self' can sometimes work against each other, giving rise to cognitive dissonance, which Oxford Languages defines as, "the state of having inconsistent thoughts, beliefs, or attitudes, especially as relating to behavioral decisions and attitude change."

From what we've learned about frequency, we know that unstable vibrations shift identity. Hypocrisy, betrayal, deception, and doubt are born from mental fluctuation. Heart arrhythmia is a physical manifestation of this principle. The HeartMath Institute studies electromagnetic fields produced by the heart. They have chosen the term "coherence" (literally 'to stick together') to describe an optimal state of health:

> *The coherence state, activated by sustained positive emotions, is associated with a highly ordered, smooth, sine-wave-like heart rhythm pattern . . . This state is termed psychophysiological coherence, because it is characterized by increased order and harmony in both our psychological (mental and emotional) and physiological (bodily) processes.*
>
> *— HeartMath Institute[31]*

In music, theoreticians use the term 'stable' to refer to notes that are consistent with their harmonic context, while others are deemed 'unstable.' We appear to live in an unstable universe. Human society is riddled with unrest. External disharmony can manifest as war, segregation, social inequity, and divisions between the 'natural' and 'artificial' world. On closer inspection however, all external divisions, insofar as they are judgements and projections, stem from internal cognitive dissonance.

> *Only the harmonious one can understand harmony.*
>
> *— Maestro Manuel Rufino*

Experiencing harmony begins with realizing one's innate unity. For this, the various aspects of 'self' must be aligned—body, mind and spirit. Buddhism addresses this through The Noble Eightfold Path:

1. Right understanding (*samma ditthi*)

2. Right thought (*samma sankappa*)

3. Right speech (*samma vaca*)

4. Right action (*samma kammanta*)

5. Right livelihood (*samma ajiva*)

6. Right effort (*samma vayama*)

7. Right mindfulness (*samma sati*)

8. Right concentration (*samma samadhi*)

Methods to accomplish holistic wellbeing vary throughout the world, with diverse traditions prescribing some combination of diet and lifestyle to cultivate balance. While cultural approaches differ superficially and ideologically, their underlying intentions are the same—to harmonize all aspects of oneself with the environment. In reality, the individual is inseparable from the environment. All things are interdependent, no matter how distant they seem to be. Would we have evolved eyes if not for the Sun?

Meditation on interdependence is a direct path to harmony, since it dissolves mental constructs which create divisions between concepts. Subjective perception is inherently biased, giving rise to attachments and beliefs which, when challenged, bring suffering. Therefore, attachment and ignorance are considered to be primary causes of suffering. The Four Noble Truths, another pillar of Buddhism, outline the process:

1. The truth of suffering

2. The causes of suffering

3. The truth of the end of suffering

4. The causes of the end of suffering

Robert Evans said, "There are three sides to every story—yours, mine, and the truth." Multiple cameras see different angles, yet the scene is one. When two people meet, it's like two cameras shooting the same scene. Typically, a person's lens is heavily filtered through dogma. When two belief systems claim seemingly incompatible things, a paradox is born. If both cannot be true, an illusion is present. Illusion is cognitive distortion, which requires mental clarity to resolve.

An illusion is impermanent, like a mirage; a transient phenomenon rather than an eternal truth. Thoughts and feelings are temporary. The body is temporary. Entire societies, planets and galaxies are temporary. By meditating on impermanence, one can better understand what (if anything) is fundamentally true.

Let's consider the statement that, 'oil and water don't mix.' From the perspective of chemistry, oil will not bond with water because their molecules remain separate. On the other hand, we 'mix' them to make salad dressing. When we ingest them, nutrients and minerals are absorbed. Both are synthesized to constitute the body, which is a unified structure. In that sense, we can say that oil and water *do* mix. Therefore, both statements are true. Oil and water *do* and *do not* mix, depending on the context.

The above example shows that two individuals could make opposing statements and both be correct. If either claims that the other is inherently *wrong*, however, they fail to see the bigger picture. A famous paradox asks, "What happens when an unstoppable force meets an immovable object?" Stubbornness, indignation, righteousness and tyranny seek to impose an inflexible mind on an equally resistant opposition. Naturally, anarchy ensues.

So many opposing worldviews leave humanity fractured and polarized. Even the fundamental balance between masculine and feminine is disturbed. Harmony requires us to resolve all conflicts. The etymology of the word resolve is 'to loosen again,' in another sense 'to release.' If the heart is tight, the body in chains and the mind in a straight-jacket, one must yield to discover the healing power of surrender.

> *God, grant me the Serenity*
> *to accept the things I cannot change,*
> *Courage to change the things I can,*
> *and Wisdom to know the difference.*
>
> — *Reinhold Niebuhr (Serenity Prayer)*

> *The training to be peaceful is very stressful.*
> — *Maestro Manuel Rufino*

The oppressed burden themselves further with pity and anger, and so they suffer twice. Such a mind cannot know peace. Lamenting the past, fearing the future—the present remains in constant turmoil.

> *As I walked out the door toward the gate that would*
> *lead to my freedom, I knew if I didn't leave my*
> *bitterness and hatred behind, I'd still be in prison.*
>
> — *Nelson Mandela*

To resent literally means 'to feel again.' How can we purely experience the present if we superimpose a memory onto it? In music, there is an approach known as bitonality in which two different sets of notes from different keys are used simultaneously. It creates a sense that two dimensions are blending into each other. Atonality does the opposite, dissolving tonal logic and tending towards chaos. These approaches push the limits of consonance ('to sound with') and dissonance ('to sound against'). When the past or future intrudes upon the present, it creates a sort of bitonal consciousness. And when we interpret life as meaningless and random, we experience atonal insanity.

Meditation on emptiness reveals the inexplicable mystery of life. It can seem frightening or pointless to face emptiness, especially if it is conflated with nothingness (nihilism). People struggle to detach from their physical belongings, let alone their deeply ingrained worldviews. Transcendence of the self through nonduality should not be mistaken for death in the mundane sense. 'Ego death' is described as a "complete loss of subjective identity,"[32] and therefore presupposes the dissolution of all psychological complexes.

> *Be at one with the dust of the earth. This is primal union.*
> *Those who have achieved this state do not distinguish*
> *between friends and enemies.*
>
> — *Lao Tzu (Tao te Ching)*

> *Dust you are, and to dust you shall return.*
>
> — *Genesis 3:19*

Of course, such lofty concepts may seem out of touch with 'real life.' They can even contribute to an inner conflict between our current sense of self and an idealized state of being. What should we do with our thoughts, feelings, and needs? How can we lead what the Tibetans call a 'precious human life'? How do we reconcile having a subjective sense of self with the notion that we are one with the universe?

It is essential to understand this principle of frequency and vibration: that all objects—all isolated thoughtforms— are vibrations holding to a frequency. If they are recognized as distinct entities (such as a cloud, a human being, or even a thought like the word 'love')—so long as they are self-contained with a beginning, middle and an end—they have a center; the center of the heart, the center of a sound, the center of a physical object. This refers to the geometric or otherwise perceived center of any entity which has an outer limit, and is the seed around which it germinates.

Just as the planet has a gravitational center holding all things to it, all objects and forms maintain integrity through their central point of origin. This center is the source of divine inspiration, the creative force of the universe which gives rise to the vibrational object. The principle of manifestation is present within everything. In this way, every point in the universe, every vibration, exists at the center of the universe from its own perspective.

Linear time is the double-edged sword of human perception. It places our existence as a flash in eternity, yet we owe to it our perception of time itself. We all receive 24 hours each day. It is equally ours to suffer or savor. Through time, we establish and dissolve all boundaries.

We can create boundaries out of fear,
or we can create boundaries out of love and freedom.

— *Maestro Manuel Rufino*

Live and let live. When we impose judgements and restrictions on each other, disharmony is born. This violates personal autonomy. And yet, no one can dictate the reaction of another. One must consent to having their buttons pushed, by neglecting to overcome personal triggers. In *The Four Agreements*, Don Miguel Ruiz emphasizes the importance of not taking things personally:

> *Nothing others do is because of you. What others say and do is a projection of their own reality, their own dream. When you are immune to the opinions and actions of others, you won't be the victim of needless suffering.*

Music and art are clear examples of this. "Not everyone is an artist," wrote Marcel Duchamp, "but everyone is a fucking critic." Our opinions can be so fickle, and our behaviors capricious. Love and hate are only a trespass apart. Since our judgements are based on perceptions of limited information, it is difficult to draw reliable conclusions about the motivations of others. From the perspective of the unconscious, even our own motivations are obscure.

> *Father, forgive them, for they know not what they do.*
>
> *— Luke 23:34*

In music, harmony refers to a series of rules that determine what is 'acceptable' when combining frequencies. These rules vary by tradition, and they change over time. Likewise, the laws of society determine what behavior is allowed. If one violates the law, they are out of harmony with it, whether the law is just or not. *Ignorantia juris non excusat*—ignorance of the law is not an excuse to violate it.

We are at once liberated and confined by the laws of nature. The structure of our ears enables us to hear, and yet confines that hearing to a narrow range. The form of the sonnet restricts the writer to 14 lines, and yet provides a sandbox in which to create. Should the poet scorn the law?

It's either the rule of law or the law of the ruler.

— Fuad Alakbarov

We must first rule ourselves, tame our vices and temper our passions. Who can hold you accountable for an inner transgression?

Let he who is without sin cast the first stone.

— John 8:7

When a person is in harmony, they maintain integrity no matter the conditions. Their wisdom is not threatened by the ignorance of others. Their love is not diminished by others' hatred.

All the darkness in the world cannot extinguish
the light of a single candle.

— St. Francis of Assisi

Of course, there will be challenges, and our light may flicker. As much as we seek to control destiny, there is the element of surprise. Many fear uncertainty. Is it naive to believe in divine providence? Is it wise to trust an incomplete science? In a way, harmony means unlearning right and wrong; transcending good and bad, friend or foe, and remaining humble.

> Who would wish regret
> in the heart of an enemy?
> For to wish regret
> in the heart of an enemy
> is to wish regret upon the world.

And who would wish
to live in a world among regrets
even if they are not our own?

In a sense, you must be selfish enough to become selfless. Then the harmony you experience within yourself can extend to include all others. Community begins with your own come-unity.

"Pax . . . In Lak'eh . . . Al Lak'en

Pax is pronounced Pash; *the letter x represents the sh sound of languages autochthonous: Mexico is pronounced* Méshico. Pash *in Mayan is the name of the month dedicated to music; this greeting means to radiate harmonious, musical waves, from the heart towards all beings in the four directions, giving it a deep cosmic meaning to the idea of peace.* In Lak'eh: *I am You;* Al Lak'en: *You are Me; Mayan mantric formula of mutual identification, the basis of true peace, to tear down the mental walls of separateness and discrimination; is the Mayan key of understanding between beings and nations. Peace* [paz] *is the word of power of the great Maestros of humanity and their disciples, as well as of the sanctuaries' initiates. Without inner peace you cannot enjoy health, goods and possessions, love, happiness, knowledge. The Mayan conception of* [pax] *enriches the meaning of that word* [paz], *which, more than a word, is a whole science and an art so little studied and appreciated. This greeting can be accompanied with music (rattle or maraca, drum, flute) as well as with song and dance. All this greeting is ritual, is festival, joy, elevation full of gratitude to the Giver of life, to the Great Spirit, eternal and infinite."*

— *Maestro Domingo* Dias *Porta*
(Suggestions for the Cosmic Rite
of the First Heaven of Quetzalcoatl)

THE BOAT

Whether or not
we ride the same boat
we share one sea
and the same wave that strikes
you will also strike me.

8

Notes Over Time:
The Definition of a Melody

Although time is not strictly linear, when processing sound, we depend on a particular relationship with time in order to hear sounds *chronologically* (from Kronos, the Greek god of time). One note comes after another. One chord comes after another. One beat of the drum comes after another. Another second ticks by. Another sunrise, another sunset.

The progression of time consists of numerous cycles. We can break a year into months, weeks, days, hours, seconds and so on—infinitely. Music works the same way. A long composition may be broken down into smaller sections (verse, chorus, bridge, refrain, etc.). In turn, these sections are sub-divided into measures, bars and beats (smaller units like seconds or minutes on a clock).

Without the stratification of sonic content over time, we would experience sound as a single unit of unseparated vibration. All vibrational possibilities would be happening at once; low and high, loud and soft. Every timbre (tone quality), pitch and rhythm would be present in an indiscriminate whole. There would be no way of distinguishing one sound from another. The law of polarity would cease to provide contrast and thus no distinct melody could emerge.

Just as white light is the combination of all the colors of the rainbow, so white noise can be defined as a combination of equally intense sound waves at all frequencies of the audio spectrum. A characteristic of noise is that it has no periodicity, and so it creates no recognizable musical pitch or tone quality, sounding rather like the static that is heard between stations of an FM radio.

— *Encyclopedia Britannica: Noise*

In order for melody to exist, one note has to come after another. That is why the definition of a melody is:

Melody = Notes over Time
M = N/T

Patterns of speech follow the same law as melody. Words come one after another. Some languages and dialects are more or less tonal depending on the culture, but they all rise and fall, start and stop. There is always a flow of breath.

Ifyousimplyblendallwaordstogetherwithoutanypauseor separationitwillbedifficulttounderstandproperlyandwill becomefatiguingfortheearandmindtoprocess.

By. Contrast. If. You. Constantly. Stop. And. Stutter. It. Will. Feel. Like. There. Is. No. Natural. Flow.

In spoken language, as in the language of music, we make use of punctuation (pauses and rests) to produce a harmonious, digestible flow of sound. The haste with which one plays or speaks creates an effect. If you rush to say something because the situation is urgent, there is a sense of immediacy. If you speak slowly and deliberately, you communicate in a calm, clear manner. This elicits a sympathetic response in the listener, to meet you in that expression. The field of ASMR (autonomous sensory meridian response) has shown that speaking in a whisper, even if the content is nonsense, can produce a sympathetic calming effect.[33]

One interesting thing about music, especially in the case of polyphonic instruments (instruments that produce more than one note at a time) is that multiple melodies can happen at once, stacked on top of each other. When a pianist plays a chord with ten fingers, ten voices are 'speaking' at once. We can process this harmoniously, without a sense of confusion or conflict between the voices.

Try saying ten words at once, or understanding ten people talking to you at the same time. Music is a vastly more complex means of communication. We can even use music to express concrete, rational ideas. For instance, a musical phrase could be chosen to mean 'open the door', and a person trained to recognize that cue would know to open the door as soon as they heard that particular sound pattern. The German composer Richard Wagner demonstrated this through leitmotifs in which particular characters in an opera were announced by recurring melodic motives. The same occurs in Prokofiev's, *Peter and the Wolf*. Morse code is another example of non-verbal sonic language.

Drums and horns have been used since ancient times to call war formations and send messages across sonic relay systems. In the African Yoruba tradition, specific rhythmic motives are used to invoke the Orixas (ancestral spirits). Church bells call people to prayer, and a dinner bell announces the gathering. These are functional sonic signals.

Speech also works this way. We recognize something by name because we have (somewhat arbitrarily) agreed to call it that. In English we call a hole in the wall a 'door,' while in France they call it a 'port' (as in 'portal'). World languages use many different sounds and symbols to express the same thing. Some cultures have words for concepts so subtle and complex that no one can properly translate them into another language. This is because concepts are understood beyond the physical sound or literal meaning of words. There are deeper connotations, cultural memories and emotional associations involved. These unspoken attributes are essential to the notions themselves.

Languages also evolve in dialogue with the natural sonic environments in which they participate, influenced by animal calls, winds, waters and the 'songs' of nature.

Music may be the activity that prepared our pre-human ancestors for speech communication and for the very cognitive, representational flexibility necessary to become humans.

— *Daniel J. Levitin*
(This Is Your Brain on Music:
The Science of a Human Obsession)

Instrumental music conveys the ineffable. Once we introduce words with explicit meaning, the brain gets involved in a different way. Non-verbal sound (especially omitting the human voice) communicates through vibration what can only be received through other forms of perceptual intelligence. Instrumental music de-emphasizes rational processes and can help extricate us from obsessive thoughts, concerns, obligations, assumptions, misunderstandings and other forms of cognitive dissonance. This can alter our way of experiencing time.

With regards to time, sound has Vertical and Horizontal aspects:

Vertical sound may be defined as: every sound heard simultaneously in a given moment. We hear the low frequencies of a truck rumbling by while we hear the sound of a person talking, the wind blowing through the leaves and a bird chirping high in the sky. All of these sounds occur at once, on top of each other in a 'vertical' sense. At the same time, each frequency is unique, occupying its particular space (frequency range). Some frequencies overlap, amplify or cancel one another. The extremes of low and high pitch as well as low and high volume are related to the vertical poles of sound. These are relative and have no ultimate beginning or end.

Each sound has a distinct identity, yet there is also a composite vibrational body of the entire moment, composed of all contemporaneous sounds. An individual sound is like an individual member of society: to some extent, he or she is unique and autonomous with a definite life of their own; on the other hand, they are inseparable from the collective like a single gear in an intricate clock.

In music, a chord is an example of a vertical structure. One basic chord type is called a triad. A triad (as the name implies) is created by stacking three notes on top of each other and playing them simultaneously. These notes are separated by an interval called a third. Thus a triad is based on three in multiple ways (these and other fundamental topics of music theory are discussed later in this book). A melody consists of a sequence of single notes, while a *chord* is a harmonic unit consisting of at least three notes at once.

Some frequencies operate in a similar range to one another. Depending on their structure they may cancel, complement or amplify other sounds (i.e. $A + -A = 0$ or $A + A = 2A$).

Constructive Interference

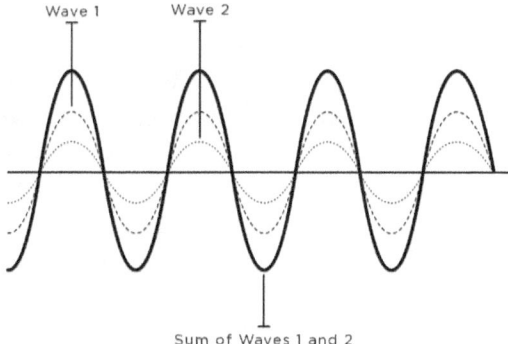

Sum of Waves 1 and 2

Destructive Interference

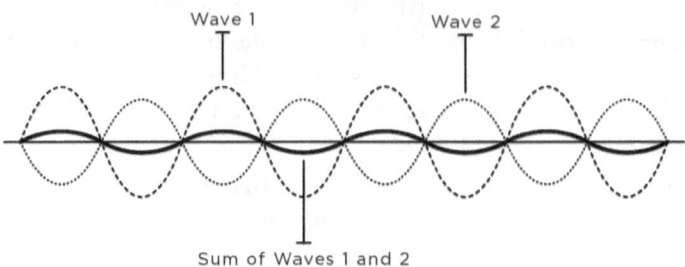

Cancellation

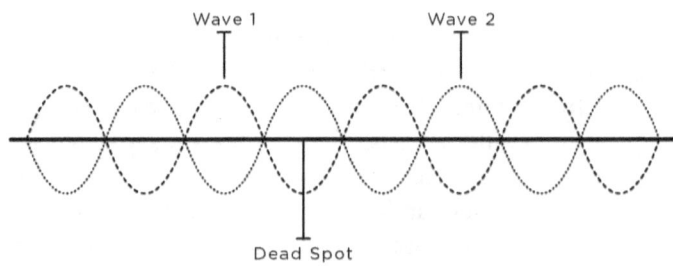

Horizontal structures, by contrast, occur one after another (sequentially rather than simultaneously). A triad can be played three notes at a time (stacked vertically), or stratified over time as three subsequent notes (horizontally). A real-word example of horizontal sound is a car door opening followed by it closing, then the key entering the ignition, the engine revving up, and driving off. These sounds occur in a progression over time.

Spoken language is a *horizontal* structure, since one word follows another. A thousand people speaking at once in Times Square is a *vertical* structure. Both aspects are interrelated and contribute to the vibratory texture we experience in a single moment, as well as over time. The main difference between them is that we perceive *horizontal* sound as occurring over time, while *vertical* sound is a moment in time.

Understanding these principles helps us listen intentionally. While attending the Eastman School of Music, a professor guided us through an exercise: "Listen to this recording all the way through. Only pay attention to the saxophone. Listen again, this time to the bass. Now, only the piano. Now the left hand of the piano. Now the right. Now the drums. Now only the snare drum, only the hi-hat, only the ride cymbal," and so on. We began to identify and isolate each individual voice contributing to the overall ambiance of the music. We also learned to hear, in a single moment, the many interacting voices (vertical).

Typically, we listen to music all at once, as a whole texture. The ear is drawn to obvious features—loud sounds, unexpected gestures, or particularly high and low frequencies. The most obvious aspects of the music tend to be the melody, bass and percussion. That's why popular music often strives to combine a catchy, memorable melody with a strong, simple bass line and a danceable rhythm. These are what most untrained ears latch onto naturally. In general, the subtler aspects of music are not consciously observed, although they are processed unconsciously. It's a case of big-picture vs. detail-oriented thinking.

From the word to the letter,
from the letter to the ink,
from the ink to the paper
to the page.

— *Yash Akasha*

Selective awareness happens all the time, as the body is constantly engaged in numerous unconscious processes that nonetheless affect us deeply (digestion, breathing, blood circulation, hand-eye coordination, etc.). It is possible to intentionally bring awareness to an otherwise automatic process. Practicing a listening exercise such as this trains the ear to discern and differentiate between many instruments, sounds and rhythms happening at any given moment.

The same principle applies to cuisine. A trained palate can taste a dish and recognize its ingredients. Most people can identify a few main ingredients, whereas a sensitive connoisseur can determine proportions, cooking times, temperatures, methods and materials used to prepare the dish. The root of the word 'connoisseur' means 'to know.'

Train yourself in the art of listening. This is a meditative practice. As you sit, notice what you hear: the hum of the refrigerator, the birds outside, the neighbor's television through the wall, your own thoughts, the sounds of your breath and body. As you walk outside, notice how many frequencies you are exposed to—thousands of sounds every single day. Acknowledge that all of these vibrations are interacting with your system. They are physically penetrating and psychically affecting you, stimulating your cells, inciting emotional reactions and causing adjustments on a molecular level. You are essentially digesting and integrating these vibrations.

By increasing awareness of the sounds you are exposed to on a daily basis, you might find yourself sensitized to things you were not sensitive to before. You may notice certain people speak loudly, or that others have a hard time hearing you even when you speak clearly. Maybe you don't need the television up so high or speakers blasting to the point that your car is rattling. Perhaps music you used to enjoy now puts you on edge, as you feel certain vibrations are loaded with angst and aggression, or that a great deal of sexual stimulation, greed and fear are being transmitted through lyrical messaging.

You may find yourself taking time in nature to be with the elements, listening to the sound of running water, or taking space from the sonic clutter of an urban environment in the relative tranquility of a forest. You may come to appreciate restorative silence which allows overstimulated senses to recover. Conversely, you may notice that the world is full of sounds you never used to pay attention to. Practicing inner silence provides more access to consciously processing everything you hear, including *what you don't realize you aren't hearing.*

Conversation was never begun at once, nor in a hurried manner. No one was quick with a question, no matter how important, and no one was pressed for an answer. A pause giving time to thought was the truly courteous way of beginning and conducting a conversation. Silence was meaningful with the Lakota, and his granting of space of silence to the speech-maker and his own moment of silence before talking was done in the practice of true politeness and regard for the rule that, 'thought comes before speech.'

— Luther Standing Bear, Oglala Chief

Selective listening is connected with selective *sounding*. As you listen deeply and understand the impact sound vibrations have on you, you develop a greater understanding of the effect they have on others. Whenever I acquire a new instrument, I experiment with it first on myself. I play it softly, loudly, close to my body, far away, near my head, near my heart, near my gut. I ask someone else to play it for me to experience it from a receiver's perspective. I notice the range of frequencies it produces (including overtones and harmonics) and how those vibrations interact with my physical and emotional body. That way I know what a listener might experience as I approach them. I study how something sounds and feels from as many vantage points as possible.

Spatial awareness is critical to anyone who works with sound. What volume is required to fill a space or make an object resonate? How can I project to direct my voice across a room, or narrow the focus on a specific person or body part? Physical space is highly responsive and dynamic. Resonance is affected by density and humidity. An instrument will sound different on a humid day than on a dry one, and a room full of bodies is softer and more muffled than an empty one in which frequencies are bouncing off of glass, wood, metal and stone rather than being absorbed by human flesh, blankets and curtains.

Each point in a room is unique in its orientation to these reflecting, reverberating waves. Each point is its own center.

The way you experience sound from your physical position and psycho-acoustic perspective differs vastly from a listener in front of, next to, above, below or behind you. Put yourself in their position. Practice being a listener. Attend sound baths and concerts as a guest. Explore your world with ears and indeed all senses open to perceiving the vibratory impact of everything within and around you.

Melodies rise and fall, start and stop. These climaxes and denouements appear like peaks and valleys of a mountain range. As we experience sound in space and time, many variables condition our perceptions. Understanding the vertical and horizontal properties of sound can lead to greater awareness of how they might be affecting ourselves and others in the moment and over time.

9

What is Sound Healing? The Art of Balancing Vibration

Sound healing is a broad term that encompasses a variety of contemporary and traditional modalities. Sound baths, guided meditation, ecstatic dance, 5Rhythms, ASMR (autonomous sensory meridian response), music therapy, psychological healing, mantra recitation, chanting, prayer, storytelling, and other practices fall under this umbrella. In order to understand what is meant by 'sound healing,' we must first explore the meaning of its two primary components—*sound* and *healing*.

Sound is a form of vibration. Vibration is the movement of energy through time and space. Sound (on the gross level) travels via mechanical pressure waves. These waves are known to interact with the physical world down to the atomic level. Atoms themselves vibrate and emit phonons, a unit of measurement akin to photons in the study of light. Stable wave patterns produce various frequencies, which have a wide range of effects on the environment. Although we typically think of sound as something audible, it can exist beyond the human hearing spectrum (20 - 20,000 hertz). Therefore, infrasound and ultrasound (below and above the audible range) also pertain to sound healing. Spoken and written language, internal monologue, song, and prayer are all forms of sound which can be used for healing.

Healing implies sickness, and sickness implies imbalance. Therefore, sound healing could be considered a means of 'balancing vibration' or 'balancing energy.' I prefer the term 'sound meditation' when discussing these subjects, since people who participate in sound healing experiences are not necessarily sick. They may participate recreationally, or as a means of reflecting and setting intentions for the future. Meditation is a common translation of the Sanskrit word *dhyana*, which has its roots in *dhi* (mind) and *yana* (moving). From this definition, we can see that meditation implies working with the movement, or vibration, of the mind. Through meditation we can observe, reflect, and respond to our environment with greater awareness. When we speak, our words strike the ears of listeners who internalize and interpret them. Therefore, two or more perspectives need to meet to make meaning out of sound.

From an early developmental stage, our minds form ideas about reality based on the words of others, and our observations of how people communicate shape our personal communication styles. The emotions associated with these interactions contribute to our understanding of truth, justice, self- preservation, and self-expression. Therefore, sound meditation begins with listening. The art of language expressed through literature, film, and music are reflections of this meditative process, further influencing our aesthetics and philosophies.

Sound meditation is ancient. Chants, prayers and songs have existed since prehistoric times, helping people make sense of life and establish a connection between the human mind and higher consciousness, or let's say: the organizing principle of the universe. Different linguistic structures underpin human interaction, shaping culture where individual and collective perspectives meet. These cultural definitions help us form an understanding of reality via cosmology, morality, academia, and so on. When things are not thoroughly meditated, confusion and deception arise, including both self-deception and the willful or unintended deception of others (e.g., propaganda, cognitive disorders, etc.). Dispelling ignorance, illusion, and negative thoughtforms are a primary function of sound meditation.

Diverse cultures have established an astounding variety of methods and protocols for facilitating sound meditation experiences. Although I prefer 'meditation,' the term 'healing' is widespread, and therefore I continue to use it in contexts where sound is applied to improve mental, emotional and physical health. Today, the world of sonic therapy can be divided into three fundamental categories, which may or may not require formal training or certification:

1. Traditional and indigenous methods

2. Empirical science-based, physiologically oriented treatment

3. Experimental and intuitive approaches

While these categories are distinct, they share some essential elements. For one, a person who is facilitating a healing has the intention to help someone heal, and the recipient has an intention to be healed. Only then can two or more people engage in a fully consensual healing process. Once the 'healer-patient' relationship is established, a 'container' is created in which treatment can occur. This could be a hospital room, psychologist's office, traditional ceremonial center, or any space chosen for the procedure—including distance healing and virtual experiences.

Image taken at a 'Sound Bath', a guided meditation experience involving multisensory healing techniques.

Innumerable instruments are used for sound meditation, some of the most common being the human voice, drums, rattles, flutes, chimes, Himalayan and crystal singing bowls, gongs, tuning forks, harmoniums and shruti boxes, didgeridoos, stringed instruments and more. These are the scalpels and anesthetics of a sound healing facilitator. Today, electronic instruments and body scanning technologies are also used to administer specific frequencies and measure electromagnetic responses throughout the brain and body. Beyond human technology, sound meditation can also involve environmental sounds such as wind, rain, thunder, ocean waves, fire crackling, animal calls and various sources of noise (such as white noise machines). Furthermore, many sound meditations involve a variety of vibrational therapies including candle light, herbs, perfumes, and other sensory factors which contribute to the atmosphere of the experience.

Some tools and instruments used for sound healing

Sound meditation is not merely a passive process. It may involve a person actively using their voice, playing instruments, or focusing the mind on specific thoughtforms such as mantras, affirmations or subjects of contemplation (e.g., impermanence or the nature of the self). Many people suffer from self-destructive beliefs, and feel inhibited when trying to express themselves, especially through song, public speaking, or in various social interactions. They may feel restricted when it comes to sharing thoughts and feelings with friends, coworkers or loved ones. Chanting (i.e., 'sounding,' or 'toning') is a powerful means of overcoming fear, shame, and self-consciousness surrounding the use of one's voice to communicate with others. Talk therapy, vocal workshops, and communication courses can help improve this area of life.

Nana Marina Cruz is a spiritual guide of the Mayan Tz'utujil people in Guatemala (or 'Guatemaya' as some prefer to call it), and a spokesperson of her tradition. She shares, "When sound, music and words are inspired from the inside out, it fills you with deep gratitude. It is a way to heal by opening your voice."

The vast world of sound cannot be easily distilled in words. There are so many intricacies and cultural considerations to take into account. For instance, in the Hindu tradition, raags (aka ragas) are not simply 'songs,' although the Western ear might interpret them as such. These ancient melodies and musical forms come with many instructions, such as the time of day or season when they are to be invoked. In Traditional Tibetan Medicine (TTS or *Sowa Rigpa*), patients are sometimes prescribed specific mantras to recite a precise number of times, in conjunction with dietary requirements. In various spiritual traditions, chants and calls to prayer occur at certain times on specific days, and may be forbidden to be used at any other time. This is not superstitiously motivated. Just as radiation must be regulated in cancer treatment, these vibrational therapies are carefully administered and monitored by traditions under the guidance of qualified practitioners.

When indigenous people speak on these subjects, it may be so foreign to our ears that it can sound whimsical or abstract. We tend to seek empirical evidence, but if we acknowledge that indigenous wisdom-keepers are trained representatives of time-tested traditions, we can better appreciate the wisdom they share. Tito la Rosa is a widely recognized master of sound healing from the Peruvian Sacred Valley, and he offers this perspective:

"Sound as a luminous vibration can regenerate your cells, organize them, make them vibrate in harmony, remind them of their function. Sound . . . can communicate with your cells and it can heal; transform. But above all, in the School of Sound in Peru, we consider sound to be an expression of love, something magic that permits you to live a transforming, luminous experience. Also, we link sound with the sacred *Chakana*, which is the organizer of the universe."

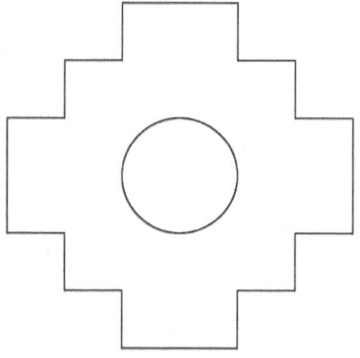

The Chakana or 'fixed cross' of the Andean cosmology is a multi-faceted symbol embedded with layers of significance. Similar archetypal geometries are found around the world.

These concepts evoke technologies such as genetic modification and infrasound therapy, but also the artful, therapeutic qualities of human expression. They speak to the nature of the universe as a fundamentally vibratory phenomenon. From that perspective, we can see that modern science and ancient spirituality are engaged in a similar conversation— exploring the primal power of sound.

Sound and silence (speaking and listening) are the basic ingredients of harmony, giving rise to action and reaction. How you behave towards yourself and others is an indication of physical, mental and emotional balance. Sound meditation encourages finding the most harmonious way to interact with the world, beyond daily conflict and the apparent contradictions of good and bad; right and wrong. What is harmonious for one is not necessarily harmonious for another. Therefore, sound healing is context-dependent. It is not a one-size-fits-all, over-the-counter medicine. Each person must explore the vast resources available, and determine what practices and sonic diet are best for them. The fundamental goal of sound meditation is to help a person return to complete alignment of mind, body and spirit; to a state of presence beyond the impermanent suffering of human experience.

10

ETHICS OF SOUND HEALING:
RESONATING WITH INTENTION

*There are sounds to open, sounds to affirm, sounds to walk
and sounds to close; a sound to search, a sound to return.*

— *Tito la Rosa*

What is the difference between a teacher, a preacher, a counselor
and a messenger?

When it comes to sound healing and meditation, people
come with a wide array of ideologies, beliefs, practices,
disciplines, experiences and personalities. It is safe to assume we
know very little regarding this vast body of human knowledge.
Sound healing, meditation, chanting and invocation are ancient
spiritual sciences; technologies that have been highly developed
in myriad forms by diverse cultures. Sound healing instruments
and practices are nothing less than sophisticated surgical tools
in the hands of a qualified facilitator.

Although sound-based therapies are receiving a lot of
attention, there are many shallow fads, overinflated egos and
dogmatic methods taking root. Sound baths have become
lucrative events where untrained opportunists are selling
sound healing services to people who are in some cases deeply
suffering and in need of psychological, emotional and physical
help. As a facilitator, you have people's lives in your hands. This
work needs to be treated with a great deal of respect, humility,
sensitivity and awareness.

Sound healing is not like grabbing a box of Tylenol off the shelf. You can't insert mantras into the ear like an over-the-counter suppository and expect it to do much more than temporarily ease someone's stress (although this is beneficial to some degree). Your inner relationship to the process is absolutely essential.

> *It depends what a person has on the inside*
> *as to what he is going to give out.*
>
> — *Dr. Jensen (Color, Music and Vibration)*

In a sense, you are not a healer. People heal themselves. They are on their own profound journeys as souls and spiritual beings across space and time. For some brief period, they have found their way to you and chosen by their own consent to engage with you in a process they believe will help them. They trust you and your intentions. They trust your knowledge and experience.

Healers may encounter people who have a tendency to seek healing from others as if it were a commodity. They go to healers without being willing to do the necessary inner work themselves and come to depend on external therapies.

> *You are looking for a good doctor.*
> *I am looking for a good patient.*
>
> — *Dr. Jensen (Color, Music and Vibration)*

Spirituality is not a business. That doesn't mean you shouldn't be able to make a living helping people and doing what you feel called to do, but as soon as your desire for profit eclipses your willingness to help people—even if that sometimes means for free—you're going in the wrong direction. Especially in the early stages, training and experience are essential. Volunteer at a school, senior home, prison or hospital. Just because you know how to package and market services doesn't mean there's any real power, depth, or knowledge behind what you offer. If you're deceiving others, you're certainly deceiving yourself. They are as ready to buy spirituality as you are to sell it. Don't sell them a lemon.

> *A fool is happy as long as his evil deed has not ripened;*
> *but when his foolishness has ripened, then does the evil-*
> *doer see evil . . . Let no man think lightly of evil, saying*
> *in his heart, It will not come nigh unto me. Even by*
> *the falling of water-drops a water-pot is filled; the fool*
> *becomes full of evil, even if he gathers it little by little.*
>
> — *Gautama Buddha (The Dhammapada)*

The most flashy, best marketed products are rarely the ones professionals use and trust, even if they appeal to the masses. This is not a popularity contest. Neither does your training as a musician, or your knowledge about sacred geometry and chakras make you any better than someone whose voice you think is bad and untrained. A sound meditation is not a conservatory environment. All the music theory and technocratic skill in the world will not equip you to meaningfully connect with the heart of a person who is coming to you with painful, complex issues that touch the essence of human suffering and experience.

This work requires more knowledge of the inner workings of consciousness than any technical knowledge of how to play an instrument or sing a sacred song. I've conducted 'sound healing' sessions where people come to me and share about sex and drug addiction, depression, family problems, physical maladies and psychological disorders. I am careful not to advise things I am not qualified to endorse. I am also willing to recommend that individuals seek help in ways I cannot necessarily provide. I am not greedy for the person to be my client. I don't want to keep them sick because it means more work for me. I am happiest when a person never comes back because they have found peace.

On the other hand, I do not underestimate my capacity to help others. I do not diminish the efficacy of this work because of any dogmas or false views held by scientific or religious communities. I do not infect my trust with the slander of taboo or the cheapness of ridicule. I strive to treat myself and everyone I encounter as sacred. In order to do that, I dedicate my life to discovering what it means to live a sacred life. Recognize the difference between temporary pain relief and a preventative practice that addresses the root cause of suffering.

My best advice to you is to let go. Let go of what you think you know. Let go of who you think a person is and what they need. Begin to *listen* with your heart. Allow your intuition to speak. Do not fall into habits, patterns or formulas of how a sound meditation experience is 'supposed' to look and sound. Some people require quiet, gentle energy and few words. Others are compelled to talk for hours. The talking may take more time during a session than the music. This too is sound healing through the power of language: mantra, prayer, reason and affirmation. Some people benefit from loud, vigorous drumming while others need flutes and breath, herbs and scented waters to comfort their senses.

The more knowledge and tools you have at your disposal, the better equipped you will be to handle a wide range of imbalances. It's important to learn as much as you can, to study traditions, ancient texts, to learn healing modalities and gain practical experience in many settings. But as soon as you enter a new situation, remember that this is the first time you have ever experienced it. This is the first time you have helped this person, even if you've seen them a dozen times. They are not the same today as they were yesterday. Allow yourselves to transform, to be fresh. Try to learn as much as you did the first time you connected with sound meditation, before you had any idea what it means to be a sound healer.

This is not a purely intellectual process. Although *The Kybalion* declares, "the universe is mental," it is tricky for our modern world to understand what is meant by 'mental' and to involve the heart with this. What is the role of the heart in relationship to the mind? Can they be unified, or must they necessarily fulfill different functions? My teacher once told me, "It is one thing to say thank you, it is another to be grateful."

Have your words become automatic? Words alone cannot carry the weight or express the depth of a heartfelt sentiment. The essence of sound healing is to embody, radiate and transmit consciousness. The key lies in cultivating one's own consciousness and sharing the benefits of that work with others, who in turn reflect the process back to you.

By contrast, pure empathy, channeling and false ideas of 'my truth' find their way into spiritual delusion. Intuition is often conflated with instinct, and fantasies are easily mistaken for visions. Therefore, reason and intuition protect each other. Love without wisdom is romantic, idealistic, purely emotional. Knowledge without love is technical, dogmatic, purely intellectual. Both imbalances are dangerous, potentially influencing an array of hyper-empathic and psychopathic tendencies.

> *We need to put wisdom in the heart,*
> *and we need to put love in wisdom.*
> *Knowledge without love leads to arrogance.*
> *Power without love leads to cruelty.*
>
> *— Maestro Manuel Rufino*

Both empathy and detachment are useful to an intuitive healer (detachment does not imply a lack of care or attentiveness, but a disidentification from the projections of others). Left and right-brain thinking (i.e. masculine and feminine qualities) are inherent in all people. In some cases, certain traits are exaggerated. Healing work—which is balance and meditation—helps to harmonize this basic internal division. Some people require more extreme recalibration than others.

> *It is perfectly conceivable to compare ourselves to a radio set, but we should realize that it is not enough to have a set for listening to music alone (just as it is not enough simply to have a body in order to make contact with the Divine); we need to plug in the set (to awaken the Kundalini current), then Light appears immediately (both in the figurative sense with respect to the human being, and in the actual sense for the radio set). After that, one needs to find the emitting station desired in order to receive its music, and having done so, the antenna of the radio set must be adjusted in the right way to have its maximum receptivity (once the body is in a state of receptivity, the chakras become condensers).*

> — Dr. Serge Reynaud de la Ferrier (Yug, Yoga, Yoghismo)

It's easy to fall into the trap of believing that because we have some special healing talent, we are somehow spiritually evolved. Do not mistake skill for realization. Any sense of spiritual superiority goes against healing. Experience can be insidious when expertise leads to pedantry rather than curiosity. We are all teachers and students. Maestro Manuel Rufino reminds me, "I know very little. Sometimes (very rarely) I am a teacher. In the house of my teacher, I am a student."

Sound healing is not a quest to be the greatest, wisest, deepest, most spiritual person in the cosmos. The humility required for this process is a vital asset. Only through humility will you continue to be willing to learn. Only through bowing to the possibility that others may know something you don't, can doors open to those teachings.

In order to understand, you have to stand under.
Otherwise, you will never understand.

— Maestro Manuel Rufino

People who consider themselves to be spiritual often toss around terms very casually. We speak of the soul, mind, heart, ego, consciousness, spirit and emotions from our current level of understanding. Sound is powerful because it has the capacity to affect all of these levels, without needing to rationalize or compartmentalize them. As a facilitator of meditation and healing, the goal is not merely to explain things the way *you* understand them, but to help others discover in themselves the relationship between all things, and to become more integrated people. This in turn will bring you insight. Their reflections are part of your own learning process. That is why it is said:

When the student is ready, the teacher will appear.
When the teacher is ready, the student will appear.

— Unknown

We benefit each other. Recognizing oneself as a student, even when in the role of a 'teacher,' is a practice of humility through service, that will help counteract arrogant and complacent attitudes regarding one's assumed knowledge. Yet, do not hesitate or doubt yourself when knowledge and intuition are truly present. Just remember that everyone's path is unique. Your path is not their path, although we are all united in the pursuit of peace.

Look at every path closely and deliberately.
Does this path have heart?
If it does, the path is good; if it doesn't, it is of no use.

— Carlos Castaneda (The Teachings of Don Juan)

11

The Functions of Sound and Music

To every thing there is a season,
and a time to every purpose under heaven:
a time to be born, and a time to die;
a time to plant, and a time to pluck up that which is planted;
a time to kill, and a time to heal;
a time to break down, and a time to build up;
a time to weep, and a time to laugh;
a time to mourn, and a time to dance;
a time to cast away stones, and a time to gather stones together;
a time to embrace, and a time to refrain from embracing;
a time to get, and a time to lose;
a time to keep, and a time to cast away;
a time to rend, and a time to sew;
a time to keep silence, and a time to speak;
a time to love, and a time to hate;
a time of war, and a time of peace.

— Ecclesiastes, 3:1-3:8

Sound is in constant dialogue with its environment, responding to countless factors including time of day, atmospheric conditions, to whom or what a sound is addressed and the customs of the space. In the case of music, there are different forms for different functions. That which is appropriate for a dance party may not be appropriate for a funeral (although some cultures joyfully celebrate the passing of a loved one).

Music for entertainment accounts for a narrow cross-section of music at large. Many influential composers, such as J.S. Bach, were commissioned to compose entirely for religious functions through the church, while others such as Mozart were appointed as court musicians by royalty seeking political prestige. Their commissions ranged from compositions welcoming honored guests to accompanying hunting parties.

Throughout history, folk music has existed as a parallel tradition alongside music of the 'elites.' Whether this elite was of a priestly, political or other social class, their preferences often differed from the music of the popular culture. In many cases, music for the elites was exclusive to the palace, courtroom or banquet and withheld from the general public. In that sense, music was democratized when concerts were brought to the stage at a ticket price the general population could afford. Artists could make a living directly from the support of audiences in an environment that was more prestigious than street or bar performances. They would not have to compose according to the demands of private commission, but rather to please society at large.

However, the stage has its drawbacks. In general, it is a form of entertainment observed by a seated, silent audience. In many cases dancing became taboo. The separation of audience and performer has resulted in many distorted perceptions of talent and artistry. It has also bred the superficial idolization of celebrities, and attitudes of superiority surrounding passing fads. Critics, producers and influencers continue to shape the art world by exalting some forms of expression while deriding others.

Many movements in music were ostracized, vilified and in some cases forbidden entirely (as in the case of blues, jazz, folk and rock and roll which were opposed by religious moral groups and dictatorships in various contexts). For thirty-two years Henry Anslinger, the commissioner of the U.S. Treasury Department's Federal Bureau of Narcotics, shaped federal law, as well as public perception of drug culture, through consistent statements like, "Most [marijuana smokers] are Negroes, Hispanics, Filipinos, and entertainers. Their Satanic music, jazz and swing, result from marijuana usage. This marijuana causes white women to seek sexual relations with Negroes, entertainers and any others."[34]

Music has been used as a means of social control and cultural homogenization, as in the case of patriotic anthems and communist songs performed by massive unison choirs to reinforce political objectives and social ideologies. Some early forms of music notation were developed under the reign of Charlemagne as he sought to employ liturgical canons of hymns as a means of establishing a unified society from formerly distinct cultural groups.

In the Catholic tradition, there is music for Mass performed traditionally on Sundays (a day of rest and prayer). In the Muslim tradition, there are calls to prayer that coincide with specific astral moments of the day including: (1) dawn, before sunrise (2) midday, after the sun passes its highest (3) the late part of the afternoon (4) just after sunset (5) between sunset and midnight. In the Jewish tradition, there are songs specific to each festivity, and times when it is strictly forbidden to play instruments or sing. There are spoken blessings over food and water. In Buddhist culture, mantras are used as invocations, to focus meditation, for specific healings as well as to recite and memorize teachings. There are Hindu traditions of chanting precise repetitions of mantras, sometimes hundreds of thousands of times to harmonize with certain astronomical factors affecting one's life. Native people throughout the world use ancient songs and melodies in an incredible array of ceremonies ranging from temazcales (sweat lodges) to tipis, Sun Dances, Moon Dances, preparations for planting and harvesting, childbirth and practically any significant daily or lifetime event, initiation or rite of passage you can imagine.

In the modern world, we find music nearly everywhere we go: in elevators, cars, stores, on television programs and portable devices which connect us with a constantly expanding library of music from around the world. Pop trends reflect cultural attitudes. Music adored by the youth epitomizes a generation. We are united by anthems. Birthdays, parties and other milestones are often enriched by music and dance, which is rhythm made visible.

It is clear that music is a fundamental branch of human expression. A Zimbabwean proverb teaches:

> *If you can talk, you can sing.*
> *If you can walk, you can dance.*

Many cultures have stifled this natural freedom of expression with shame, taboo and violent forms of repression. This disempowers people from participating in song and dance.

It is worth considering the impact of social and governmental investment in the arts and arts education on public and private life, as well as ingrained attitudes regarding the so-called 'starving artist.' It is time for the thriving artist. There is a vast and growing body of evidence illustrating that music education improves academic performance and offers many benefits in terms of emotional well-being, mental processing, overall creativity and arguably the health of culture itself.[35] What is the relationship between music and quality of life? Just because something is priceless doesn't mean it shouldn't be supported financially.

Inclusivity and exclusivity manifest in many ways for many reasons, some of which are natural and without ill-intent. There can be unity in diversity. However, if institutional poverty prevents instruments, technology and music education from reaching certain demographics of the population, we need to actively address those inequities. Likewise, if one cultural group's artistic standard imposes itself on another, we must become more open-minded and willing to appreciate unfamiliar traditions.

*   *   *

Human beings employ not only music, but sound in general with a high degree of intention. There are dial tones for phones, sirens for emergency vehicles, audible walk signals for the blind and countless electrical beeps and cues that tell us when the stove is hot, when the laundry is done, when the kettle has boiled and so on. It would be inappropriate for an emergency alarm to sound when nothing is wrong, just as it would be out of place to hear a cell phone ring in a library. Context is key.

With modern technology and mass communication, vibrations travel from earth to satellites and back again, broadcasting worldwide simultaneously. These signal blankets reach remote oceans and deserts, resulting in an increasingly globalized culture (as well as unintended consequences in nature when frequency transmissions adversely impact animal communication). Many of the unique quirks of regional dialects have been lost through homogenization in the mainstream. Nevertheless, the essential utility of language and sound remains clear.

The linguist Noam Chomsky explores the root structures of world languages, suggesting that while forms may change (vocabulary, colloquialisms, dialectical features, etc.) their functions remain the same (noun, verb, adjective, preposition, etc.).

A language is not just words.
It's a culture, a tradition, a unification of a community,
a whole history that creates what a community is.
It's all embodied in a language.

— *Noam Chomsky*

The words and expressions we choose are situational. People tend to address a friend differently than a lover, boss, child or mother. People have individual ways of communicating with a pet. One should be deeply aware of context and whom one is addressing when deciding with what tone and diction to speak. Sometimes silence is the most appropriate response.

Do not speak recklessly or superficially. With a few words, previously meditated, much may be said. On the contrary, the one who speaks much, says little. The silence of meditation and study allows us to choose the most just and defined words according to the situation . . . It is the alchemy of sound, where words resonate as mantras if they are accompanied by silence. A musical composition without silence is converted into noise.

— *Maestro Domingo Dias Porta*

Recognizing the distinct function of sound and music in various contexts frees us from unnecessary comparisons. Sometimes people argue that one artist is objectively better than another—that their music is more sophisticated or beautiful— but when you look at the time and purpose for which it was composed, by whom and for what audience, you realize that all art responds perfectly to its niche. There is no need to compare things in terms of subjective opinion or value.

In the context of sound meditation, sometimes the atmosphere calls for calming, energizing, triggering memory, stimulating the heart, activating the breath or grounding. These functions are only a few among many. Understanding your listener and the needs of your environment will enable you to converse more naturally through sound. You will intuit how to project to properly fill a space, and what to express in order to harmonize the space.

Thought inspires action. It is clear that ideas can change the course of humanity. Words written thousands of years ago continue to impact human belief systems. Ancient music influences modern composition.

One of the salient functions of music and language is its capacity to communicate not only rationally, but abstractly and with emotion. Expressing love is a function of sound. Inauthentic people say the right words but lack conviction. A perfectly reasonable idea expressed with poor taste and timing will offend someone (politics and religion are controversial dinner guests). A sloppily executed punchline leaves an audience dead in their seats, and a hastily formulated thought is unconvincing.

Each person articulates based on their focus and level of awareness. Emotional intelligence is a measure of one's capacity to express themselves harmoniously, to be responsible with words and actions, and to be sensitive to the environment. Outbursts are unintentional. They are automatic fight or flight response mechanisms. Therefore, controlling one's word choice, tone of voice, volume and emotional charge can transform conflict into resolution.

Oftentimes we don't realize the impact of our words, spoken or unspoken. Nevertheless they have consequences, whether conscious or unconscious, intended or unintended, beneficial or detrimental. This is not to say we are responsible for the opinions or reactions of others, but one thing is certain: the vibrations we generate transform life from the inside out, like a drop of food coloring added to a swirling glass of water. We can pollute those waters with negative thoughts, words and actions, or we can purify them with peace and compassion. We can put up walls with words or with silence. As a ship's course is changed by the turn of a sail, or a chariot steered by the pull of the reins, destiny is altered by discipline. A person of restraint is spared the consequences of reckless emotional behavior. When obstacles come, they are taken in stride. The wind still blows, but now it must travel by another path.

In the natural world, sound has countless functions. There are calls to warn of danger, mating calls, sounds to locate family and so on. Bernie Krause has been studying soundscape ecology for decades. His research categorizes sound into:

1. Geophony (sounds from non-biological sources)
2. Biophony (sounds from biological sources)
3. Anthrophony (sounds from human-made sources)

In one case study he postulates that certain species of frog croak in synchronicity to make it harder for predators to isolate them as prey. Examining spectrograms (visual renderings of recorded sound) illustrates how diverse species coexist sonically to communicate in dense biospheres such as the Amazon rainforest, and how they can be adversely impacted by noise pollution from anthrophonic sources such as airplanes and logging. Every sound occupies a bandwidth. Nature makes use of rhythm and balance to ensure that each bandwidth is unimpeded by obtrusive sounds. Oversaturation of a certain bandwidth means communication will be more competitive within that range.

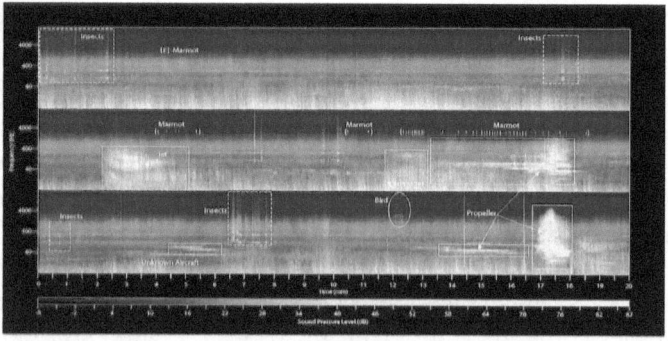

A spectrogram renders sound in a graph. High and low frequencies are on the vertical access while time is the horizontal access.

Sound can have creative, nourishing, or destructive impacts. Interference is an example of a destructive wave pattern, whereas sympathetic resonance can be seen as a strengthening force. In Hinduism, Brahma, Vishnu and Shiva represent the creator, sustainer and destroyer of the universe. When working with sound, consider what is being created, reinforced, or de-emphasized by a given vibration.

In any ecosystem, many functions are performed with local and global impacts. The smallest gear of a watch is no less important than the largest. A small shift can cause a massive avalanche. Do not underestimate the potential impact of a word or action. It is easy to overlook details and disregard minutia as inconsequential, but nature reveals that even the smallest seed can become a forest.

Functions are not singular. A cloud not only dispenses rain, but collects it as well. It provides shade. It shapeshifts with the imagination of a child. It reflects the light of the sun, traps warmth from escaping into the open atmosphere and extends the beauty of sunset. Is beauty not functional? Design is not merely practical. A song that kindles love in the heart of one may painfully recall loss in another. At times, function is subject to personal interpretation. This is why one's intentions have a significant influence on the impact of an action, and why it's not always enough to 'mean well.'

The road to hell is paved with good intentions.

— *Proverb*

Intention is central to the creative process, like making a storyboard before the film. It's hard to know how your choices will resonate with others without knowing their triggers, predispositions, cultural expectations and so on. A simple hand gesture performed in a foreign country can offend someone without your knowing. Making a 'V' with the index and middle fingers means peace, military victory, or a curse depending on whom you're addressing. Form and function are subject to interpretation.

12

The Lifecycle of a Sound: Entrance, Sustain, and Release

The production of sound involves three fundamental stages:

1. Entrance
2. Sustain
3. Release

Entrance refers to the way a sound is entered from silence. Whether produced by striking a string, drum or bowl, passing air through the vocal cords to produce vibration, or any other means of giving rise through movement to sound, the entrance is its beginning—the inception of the audible. A sound's entrance may be gentle, soft, subtle, breathy, crisp, firm, hard, clear or sudden. These are examples of different types of *articulations*. In traditional European classical music theory, terms such as *staccato* and *legato* are used to describe short and long articulations.

Sustain refers to the duration of a sound once it has been produced. A singer may hold a long note, or a guitar string may return back to silence (decay) as it resonates. The length of time a sound endures is related to its sustain. Volume, tone, timbre and other sonic elements may be manipulated during the period of the sustain.

Release refers to how the sound is dissolved back into silence. Whether by a clear, abrupt cutoff or a gradual fade of volume, eventually the sound will cease to be audible. The articulation of a cutoff book-ends the entrance.

Entrance (also known as attack), *sustain* and *release* are essential sonic elements to be aware of. Even so, there is a 'silent' inner process of preparation for any entrance which is equally important. Our intentions presuppose our actions. It's like dropping a pebble into a pond. After a sound is produced, it continues to resonate throughout time and space. The splash lasts for a moment, but the ripples extend far beyond. There is no definite beginning or end. Rather, phenomena emerge from and return to an unbroken continuum (just as waves rising and falling on the surface are reabsorbed endlessly into a body of water).

Sound waves have a tangible impact on the waters of the body. The energetic currents that run through us can be shifted. The impacts of this extend far into the future. A person whose vibrations are altered by sound may leave a space with a completely different inner state than how they entered. They can arrive stressed-out and high-strung, then depart in tranquility. This residually affects the thoughts they think and emotions they feel as they continue on their way, which will in turn alter how they interact with others. Those changed interactions can produce a cascading reaction of harmony. From the inside out, your capacity to generate peaceful, harmonious vibrations can bring harmony to the entire world (poignantly expressed in the film *Pay it Forward*). In chaos theory, the *butterfly effect* suggests that an insect flapping its wings across the ocean contributes to the winds which become a hurricane thousands of miles away. This is not just a dramatic metaphor, but an acknowledgement that all things are deeply and subtly interconnected; essentially interdependent.

We know that the moon's gravitational impact sways the entire ocean. Within human beings it affects menstrual cycles, and statistics show that violent crimes increase during the three day full moon period. Legend tells of the werewolf emerging under a full moon, as man succumbs to his animal nature and forgets who he is until the dawning sun returns. In many traditions, water is associated with emotion. We shed tears. We become hot-blooded. We are flooded with and carried away by emotion.

Water is a cleanser and purifier. We are largely composed of water. Drinking water nourishes our cells and helps detoxify the entire system. Every cell of the body and the DNA itself are pervaded with water. Because sound travels through water, it is clear that sound can be used to impact the molecular structure of bodily fluids.

Sounds have a natural life cycle like our own birth (entrance), life (sustain) and death (release), echoed by the inhale, turning point and exhale of the breath. Wind instruments (flutes, voice, brass instruments, didgeridoo, etc.) are especially connected with the breath. They require keen control of the muscle groups, bandhas and diaphragms that regulate airflow in the body. In general, musical phrases, like speech, follow the natural human lung capacity. Pauses are taken to recover the breath. These punctuations also give the ear and mind a moment of rest, to process information and prepare to respond or receive more content.

Certain instruments, however, are able to sustain indefinitely. Circular breathing refers to the process by which a person exhales air stored in the mouth while at the same time drawing in new air through the nose, allowing them to send air out while inhaling at the same time. This technique is essential to playing some drone instruments.

A continuous, uninterrupted sound is called a drone. There are many droning instruments, including the didgeridoo, shruti box, harmonium, Himalayan singing bowls, electric synthesizers, bagpipes, and can also include bowed instruments such as the violin, viola, cello, arco bass, etc.

Droning instruments are unique in that there is no pause between phrases. A continuous bed of sound is produced. This can stand alone or serve as a foundation for a chant or other melodic statement. This steady sound can have an effect similar to white noise, which some find comforting and helpful for sleep. Binaural beats, electric fans and nature soundscapes such as rivers and wind all produce this effect of constant ambient sound.

Percussion instruments in general have very little sustain by comparison. Typically, a drum produces a short, striking sound. It quickly fades before it needs to be struck again. Instruments such as the djembe, cajon, drumset (not including cymbals), dumbek, frame drum, and countless others from around the world, offer a strong emphasis on the element of entrance or *attack*.

Many instruments fall somewhere in between. The acoustic guitar is sounded by strumming, plucking or fingerpicking. Once a string has been struck it produces a sound and immediately begins to fade. Most of the volume is gone within several seconds and the instrument becomes silent within roughly ten seconds. Electric instruments may have a longer sustain, and can even generate drones due to the presence of electro-magnetic pickups and feedback loops from the amplifier.

When a sound is introduced, the way it enters space can harmonize or clash in various ways. Does a person barge into a room and call attention to themselves, or do they sneak in like a thief who doesn't want to be detected? Do they enter calmly and gracefully, or clumsily trip over the threshold? Many people lack sensitivity in this area. They either enter intrusively or, if they are timid, do not exert sufficient energy to confidently join the current, like a hesitant car trying to merge with traffic. One must gauge the vibrations already circulating and intuit the appropriate way to join in.

Various rhythms, volumes and frequency ranges are continually occupied or left open. Participating in that conversation at times requires synchronizing or unifying, and at others filling in the gaps (i.e., syncopating). Entrance, sustain, and release are the life cycle of each sound participating in this process.

These phases of sound are also present in the archetypes of stories themselves. On a large scale, they are reflected in the lifecycles of entire traditions. Christianity has been one of the most dominant traditions of the past two thousand years. When we consider its emergence, spread and decline, we can see how the lifecycle of a sound parallels large-scale cultural movements:

> Entrance: When Christ came to
> Jerusalem, his teaching presented
> a new way of approaching one's
> individual relationship to God.

> Sustain: After his departure, the
> church established doctrines to
> preserve and perpetuate his teachings.

> Release: In modern times, many
> dogmatic interpretations of scripture
> are fading from the social ethos.

Musical elements have always been interwoven with storytelling. The link between music and brain functions such as linguistic and emotional processing, motor skills and memory make music an excellent tool for multi-sensory learning. When we hear the birth, life and death of a sound, on a deeper level, we hear the expression of our own lifecycle.

13

THE SONIC JOURNEY:
HOME, DEPARTURE AND RETURN

Another archetypal trinity in music is *home*, *departure* and *return*.

Home is the sense of arrival, of rest, of where we belong. The home key (also known as the mode) or primary tonality, creates this impression. The first note we hear in a piece of music automatically orients our ears, so that anything which follows is contextualized in relationship to it. Similarly to how we orient ourselves to a star or constellation, we navigate sound by way of a central pitch or rhythm. Typically, one or two pitches (notes) will be emphasized more than any other in a piece of music.

In music that features droning instruments (shruti box, didgeridoo, sarod, etc.), sustained pitches create a foundation or underlying texture, over which a melody or mantra is layered. This type of music creates a very stable sense of home since there are few if any changes in key center or harmony. Because of this, the sense of departure and return are suggested by melody and rhythm.

Departure occurs as soon as we deviate from the established home. Once a key center, chord, or drone orients us to the tonality of the music, any element of surprise can be seen as a departure. In the case of harmonically active music, this may occur as a new chord (perhaps played by a guitar or piano) that opens us to new sonic territory. It may also occur as a change in sonic texture, instrumentation or volume. However the departure is achieved, it is clear that we are going somewhere, not simply remaining in the same energetic place. This sense of departure may be dramatic or surprising, subtle or discrete, but most often it leaves us with a sense of suspension—an intuitive understanding that we are going somewhere, that this is not the ending, and that somehow we will return home again or depart somewhere else.

Return is the axis, the point at which we reorient ourselves and it becomes clear that we are coming home or approaching a significant moment of arrival or resolution. It may occur as a climax, like the peak of a roller coaster before the descent. There is so much implied harmony and resolution in these moments that the ear has an expectation to return somewhere familiar. Usually, the return leads us back to where we started, whether that means the same chord with which we began, or a melodic phrase from earlier in the music.

Sometimes however, a return can lead to a *deceptive resolution* or *deceptive cadence*, in which another departure is exchanged for the anticipated return home. This destabilizing motion can surprise the listener and also recontextualize familiar content in unexpected ways.

It is easier to hear the principles of home, departure and return at work in popular songs, classical or traditional compositions with a clear sense of formal structure. As with poetry, there are various standard forms depending on the culture, time-period and genre.

32 Bar Song form (Jazz and American Songbook):

A (8 measures)
A (8 measures repeated perhaps with slight variation)
B (8 measures of new material)
A (8 measures of the original material returning)

12 Bar Blues:

A (4 measures)
A (4 measures repeated)
B (4 measures of new material)

CALL AND RESPONSE

Much of the music composed throughout history makes use of key centers and canonical chord progressions called paradigms, which create satisfying, predictable balances of harmonic and rhythmic motion, tension and resolution. In traditional music theory terms, these three aspects are referred to as Tonic (Home), Predominant (Departure) and Dominant (Return).

Around the turn of the 20th century, and later in response to the shock of two World Wars, a paradigm shift occurred. Composers such as Arnold Schoenberg and Anton Webern responded with music that reflected their chaotic world. Atonal music intentionally deconstructs any sense of home at a time when entire cultural groups were being displaced or having their homes literally destroyed. By treating the 12 pitches of the chromatic scale equally, any emphasis on key or tonality is intentionally avoided, producing an unstable feeling of perpetual non-arrival. Rhythms are also destabilized to avoid resolution and create a sense of endless shifting or floating. Atonal (also known as 12-tone) music may also be serialized, or mathematically ordered in a way that mirrors a manufactured, box-like expression of human logic.

Even so, home, departure and return are inherent to atonal music, since there is no way to avoid that the music has a beginning, middle and end. This arc necessitates a journey of some kind. The rising and falling of volume (dynamics) and the thickening and thinning of texture (more or fewer voices/ instruments) also contribute to this arc of intensity. Any sonic elements introduced or modified throughout the composition which catch your attention can serve as musical milestones, interpretable through the lens of home, departure and return.

Listen critically and ask yourself what you notice in a given piece of music. What sensation is created from moment to moment? Do you feel resolved? Are you left hanging or wanting more? Was some particular element surprising or unexpected? Can you predict when the music is about to end? Such cues make more sense in context and function as you begin to interpret them through these archetypal phases of home, departure, and return.

SYMMETRY

The journey away from home and back again follows a cyclical symmetry. Symmetry is a form of predictable patterning, which is satisfying to the organizational behavior of the human mind. Symmetry is expressed through sound in various ways. For example, call and response establishes symmetry reflected between the caller and the responder. Sometimes the same phrase is repeated, or a different phrase responds to the call.

More abstractly, melodic phrases can be symmetrical as well. Let's take a three note melody as an example:

A   B   C

This could be reflected symmetrically in the following ways:

A   B   C | C   B   A

or

A   B   C | A   B   C

This principle applies to both melodies and rhythms. Rhythmic symmetry is a big part of what makes it easy for even a small child to dance along with the beat of a drum. Evenly spaced drum beats are inherently symmetrical.

14

TENSION AND RESOLUTION: CONSONANCE AND DISSONANCE

It's not the note you play that's the wrong note—it's the note you play afterwards that makes it right or wrong.

— Miles Davis

In the context of sound and music, there are many ways to elicit tension and resolution. Harsh or abrasive sounds, clashing textures and vigorous strikes may cause tension in the nervous system and induce a listener to pay more attention ('at tension') to a particular aspect of sound.

Tension is accumulated anticipation over time. Tension can come suddenly (in the case of an abrupt or unexpected sound) or it can build gradually. If you ring a bell, a person will notice it immediately. Initially, they may find the sound pleasant, but if you keep ringing it, after a minute or two they'll likely want it to stop. *How long are they going to carry on?* The person has an expectation that the sound will end. This unfulfilled expectation causes tension. They are waiting for resolution.

Words that carry negative associations can also cause tension. People have all kinds of emotionally charged attachments and aversions to different sounds, instruments, songs, concepts, languages and other aspects of the world. Tension can arise in someone for reasons that are highly subjective to their unique conditioning.

Tension is eased or balanced by one's capacity to *relax* and accept, to release expectations and refrain from judgment in order to remain fully present as an unbiased observer.

In musical terms, dissonance is a cause of tension. Dissonance is the opposite of consonance, and implies disharmony. Juxtapositions of certain notes or rhythms may be considered dissonant, such as a person singing or playing 'off-key' ('off-pitch' or 'out of tune'), although these are subjective, conditional standards.

Rhythmic dissonance can also be deeply unsettling, like when a drummer plays 'out of time,' slows down or speeds up, or emphasizes an unusual part of the music. If you PLACE emphasis IN unexpected PLACES, tension and surprise are created. This applies more directly to people who understand the language (and thus have linguistic expectations) than to those for whom the idiom is foreign. If you don't understand a language to begin with, you certainly won't notice if someone is speaking incorrectly.

When dissonance is brought into consonance, there is resolution.

Resolution is the fulfillment of an expectation. It provides a sense of arrival or release, of conclusion and completion. It is more likely to result in comfortable, harmonious feelings. As a listener, this can mean surrendering to a musical journey without needing to know where it's going or when it's going to end. Resolution may also occur as a satisfying validation of what one assumes will happen next. Patterns and repeated elements are frequently employed to make things memorable. Predictability can be boring, but patterns can also be comforting. They help us organize and process information.

You already know what I'm going to say before the words come out of my . . . *mouth*.

Later, we will discuss certain ways in which music theory reveals 'implied resolution' in terms of harmony.

Tension and resolution are polarizing forces that can be seen as peaks and valleys. The push and pull of these elements creates drama, contrast, dynamism and a range of emotional expressivity with sound. Building up to a loud, rhythmically active peak before breaking down to a quiet, spacious texture is one way of building and releasing tension.

The movement from tension to resolution is a harmonizing process. Words often trace a story arc that moves from tension to resolution. This transcendental journey leads us from conflict to peace, struggle to liberation, despair to optimism, resistance to acceptance, hostility to grace. For a sound healer or meditation guide, it is important that the messages embedded in our verbal and instrumental vibrations express this potential; otherwise, we may transmit despondent, hopeless, pessimistic, apathetic, aggressive or generally negative attitudes.

Is there anything wrong with negativity or tension? Not inherently. What we are talking about is balancing these poles. A person who is too engaged with tension might develop hypertension, while a person who is too relaxed or naively blissful might become ineffective, lazy, ignorant and so on. A skilled person who is in alignment with nature knows how to navigate the ups and downs of life, when to embrace stress and how to work with it.

The nervous and immune systems are strained by anxious states yet can benefit from exposure to extreme conditions of stress and release (fasting, saunas, sweat lodges and cold plunges). Likewise, muscles can be strengthened by alternating periods of exercise and rest. In the sonic sense, moods are established according to the balance of tension and resolution. Sustained moods tend to be trancelike, while rapid shifts in texture are more emotionally dynamic.

15

TONE AND TEXTURE

Tone and texture are key components of sound. Like paint on a canvas, sounds can be layered in many ways—rough or smooth, thick or thin, subtly blended or starkly juxtaposed. By word, a house is a house, but how you *represent* it as a subject in art depends on how you interpret the concept tonally and texturally (among other variables).

In musical terms, the note 'middle C' is a fixed pitch. As a frequency, it has a standard definition (261.6 Hz), but in terms of its sonic potential, it can be as variegated as the color blue. The name doesn't tell us how a color looks or a note sounds, nor how it interacts with other sounds. What matters is how you treat it, how you express it, how you color it and contextualize it.

Tone refers to the *quality* of sound. Tones can be harsh, soft, round, bright, damp, muted or cutting to name only a few possible descriptors. One way to conceptualize tone is to imagine a parent speaking with a loving voice. Now imagine their disciplinary voice. How does someone sound when they are trying to comfort, teach, flirt or play with you? Words can be spoken in many tones that evoke different feelings and responses.

The same is true of musical notes and instruments. A melody can be played on various instruments. "Happy Birthday" could be performed on piano, guitar, trombone or voice. Even the rhythm of the melody could be represented on a non-melodic percussion instrument such as clapping or a drum. All of these instruments have different tonal qualities and properties of sound.

When monks chant the primordial sound 'Aum,' they work deeply with the principle of tone. Even if they chant one pitch for hours, they are constantly manipulating the quality of sound, discovering new ways to resonate throughout the body, and color their voice with deep states of concentration. They shape and sculpt the way frequencies are formed and direct vibrations with intentional precision to affect different chakras (energy centers with correlations to aspects of the physical, emotional, mental and subtle bodies).[36]

Volume can impact tone, but they are distinct concepts. For example, it is possible to be loud with a soft or gentle tone. It is also possible to be quiet with an abrasive or harsh tone. Listen to a song on your phone. When you turn the volume down, the tone of the music does not change substantially. You still recognize the unique quality of the singer's tone of voice, now just more quietly.

Texture is related to tone but usually refers to the interaction of multiple sounds. A 'single voice' is one instrument speaking, like a monologue in a play. As more instruments or voices are added, the texture 'thickens.' Similarly, a thicker texture can be produced on a piano or guitar by playing several notes at once. The guitar has six strings. Using all six at once is a thicker texture than selecting only two or three. Likewise the piano is used to create textures ranging from one to ten voices (one for each finger).

Nonetheless, an individual instrument or voice can still express a variety of textures. Some singers have a 'smoky' or 'raspy' voice. This relates to tone, but it is also textural. The two concepts are not completely unrelated, and sometimes a distinction between them is merely semantic. Sound, especially non-verbal sound, evades description. It speaks for itself. Nonetheless, learning to describe and communicate sound quality in terms of tone and texture makes it easier to convey ideas to others, and to explore variation in one's own sonic palette.

It is important to remember that even in a very full texture (such as an orchestral symphony or vocal choir which may have dozens of voices), each individual voice is responsible for their own unique treatment of tone. How they blend together is an artform unto itself. Practicing emulation is a way to gain mastery over the subtleties of tone. Can you imitate the vocal style of Louis Armstrong, Chet Baker or Amy Winehouse? Can you play with the same tone and rhythm as Jimi Hendrix? Can you pronounce 'Aum' like a Tibetan monk? Listen deeply and repeat what you hear as precisely as possible.

16

Mantra

Say continually that sacred name
which will make thee sacred.

— *Zeb-un-Nissa*

A common translation of 'mantra' is 'mind protection.' 'Aum' (also spelled 'om,' 'ohm,' or 'ong') is perhaps the most well-known mantra in the world, considered by many to be the primordial sound of creation. Although we reduce this sound to a few letters on a page, its pronunciation is far more nuanced.

To begin with, consider the letter 'A'. This symbol can be pronounced in many ways: hard, soft, long or short. These ways cannot be written, they must be heard and emulated. The incredible variety with which any vowel or consonant can be pronounced lends a clue to the depth of mantra practice. A subtle adjustment of the lips, mouth shape, tongue placement or other physiological structure can dramatically alter the pronunciation of a sound. Therefore 'Aum' represents an infinite vibratory spectrum. It also represents an eternal sound. Its primordial nature provides a vibratory architecture, like an ocean in which islands emerge and submerge. A mantra is like the sky, clear and stable, holding space for passing clouds.

Mantra is a Sanskrit word, deriving from ancient India.
It literally means,
'To save the mind from suffering and illness.'

— Dr. Nida Chenagtsang
(Interdependent Science of Tibetan Mantra Healing)

A mantra is made up of seed sounds and syllables which, when used in combination, are like strands of code. This code may alter physical, mental and emotional states. Due to their vibratory properties, sounds can restructure bodily fluids, molecules and cells, and impact the genetic code itself. DNA is adjustable and rewritable, as are virtually all of our imprinted patterns.

Mantra, yantra and *tantra* are some of the most misrepresented terms borrowed from Eastern spirituality. Within the context of a holistic healing system, mantra practice is accompanied by diet, visualization, mental and physical exercises, external therapies and frequency variables such as the number of repetitions, time of day and season when they are to be practiced. This is to ensure that harmony is achieved on the levels of mind, body and speech (thought and action). Depending on what level, and with what mentality one approaches healing and meditation, these principles can be taken very deeply into oneself, to the foundation from which identity emerges.

I [Krishna] am the father of the world—its mother, its arranger and its grandfather; I am what is to be known; the purifier; the sound 'Om'; the Rig, the Sama and the Yajur Veda.

— Bhagavad Gita, 9:17

In order to access the primordial, we must understand archetypes and symbols as they speak in simple, elegant terms. We must transcend the rational, intellectual mind to understand things that defy explanation in words. Thus the symbol 𝕆𝕞 (Aum), must be understood as a sort of .zip file to be unpacked within oneself.

A—U—M; the ocean its abdomen;
the moon and the sun are its eyes; the fire is its mouth;
Visnu is its heart; Brahma is its head; and Rudra is its locks.

— *V. Krishnaraj*

Primordial sound is woven into the fabric of reality. Vibration, describing oscillation through time and space, is a fundamental aspect of creation. The ancient Mayans define it as *Hunab Ku*: "the ultimate giver of movement and measure."

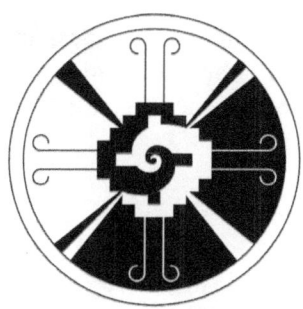

Hunab Ku ("the ultimate giver of movement and measure"),
a galactic Mayan symbol.

Different pronunciations of sounds affect their resonance internally and externally. When you close your mouth to hum, vibrations are directed inward. Human beings have many ways of targeting objects with sound waves. Ultrasound technology focuses sonic vibration like a laser focuses light. However, no external equipment is needed to direct sound with intention using the voice. Try the following exercise:

1. Pinch your nose and speak with a nasal tone, repeating the phrase: "rain ran around the river."

2. Drop the voice into the mouth, throat and chest. Keep the nose pinched. Intentionally avoid speaking into the nose and say the phrase, "Hi, how are you?"

3. Repeat, alternating between the first and second steps.

4. Notice that the speaking voice can be consciously redirected into different chambers of the body, such as the head, throat, chest, gut, etc.—anywhere within oneself or towards another.

Developing this sensitivity, awareness and precision requires physical control over the mechanisms of anatomy which manipulate sound, in conjunction with the conscious intention to project it there.

The enunciation of sound is not relegated merely to its physical, audible aspects. One can also practice silent recitation, when the inner voice speaks. Mental dialogue and emotional language also contribute to the character of sound. The vibrations that emerge from you, which you radiate and transmit, are multi-layered. You are a conduit of vibrations. Thus, learn to pronounce 'Aum,' not only with your voice, but with your entire self. Bring as much consciousness to the act as possible.

There are many teachings from throughout the ages about 'Aum' and what it represents, but in general it may be worth noting that in order to produce the sound, one must first *open*: open the throat, open the mouth and pronounce the 'open' vowel, 'A'. Next, the shape of the mouth begins to tighten and narrow to create the 'U'. Finally, it closes completely for the 'M', where the vibration turns inward—a return to its point of origin. This circular structure is an essential geometry of the universe. The relationship between giving and receiving, internal and external are also implied. It is also triadic in nature, thereby opening doors to many other associations (birth, life, death; past, present, future, etc.).

These are only some possible interpretations of 'Aum'. It is not intended to be taken as 'correct', nor sufficient in describing what is ultimately an unspeakable knowledge. Yet, it may serve to illustrate how we can approach what might otherwise be an automatic, shallow process of singing mantras and chanting.

Om is the union of all mantras.

— Drukmo Gyal

As you 'silently' read these words, a voice pronounces them in your mind. One can recite mantra with this 'silent' voice. When you reach a vibration through mantra or invocation, that state of mind becomes accessible at any time. You can evoke the nonverbal essence of the energy. The mantra has sublimated from a physical, audible, verbal form to a transcendental energetic state. Words are to a mantra what a body is to the soul—a skin, a layer, a wrapping. The essence of your being is not the body, and the essence of the mantra is not its seed syllables. Its purpose is not to be pronounced 'correctly' by some dogmatic or didactic standard, but to facilitate a connection to transcendental states of consciousness. Once this has been achieved, the mantra itself can be seen as a bridge *towards*, rather than a destination unto itself. It facilitates a connection to the higher self through yoga, or 'union with the divine.'

When you give power and energy to the mantra itself, the practice becomes religious and ritualistic. It is critical to understand that these energies are *within* you. As you come to experience them and develop the capacity to maintain and call them into being at any moment (including under the most challenging circumstances) no special mantra is needed to connect with peace itself, devotion itself, love itself and so on, although they may be helpful reminders in the interim.

The same is true of any dependency or attachment we have. So long as we feel we need crystals to illuminate our chakras, drinks to regulate our nerves, or people to validate us and feed us love, we will never be able to generate wholeness from within. Too much focus outside, on external factors such as a given mantra, prevents us from properly integrating them.

Let's break with the left brain for a moment and tap into the creative wisdom of the right hemisphere.

>Aum
>
>Home
>
>Homme (French for 'man')
>
>Um (Russian for 'mind')
>
>Solomon (*shalom*, soul of man, son of man,
>   sun and moon, only one)

Why are any sounds related? By what system of logic or other patterns do they become connected in our minds? There is value to free association. Recognize the familial nature of certain sounds:

>Roam
>
>Omen
>
>Moment

Whether they contain an identical or similar sound structure, this only indicates a lesser degree of symmetry:

>Solemn
>
>Lonesome
>
>Tomb

As one sound recalls another, the journey may lead seemingly far from its origin, yet there is a connective thread. Allowing oneself to free-associate can open new pathways and connections, creating fresh neural pathways in the brain. The process of association brings order to chaos. It brings unity and harmony to formerly disparate elements. Is this a pointless, vain, arbitrary or imagined comparison? Whether or not you think so, your mind draws connections anyway. The mind is almost constantly making associations for reasons that may be sonic, connotative, emotional, based on memory, etc.

In the Jewish tradition, there is a careful emphasis placed on acknowledging the unknowable, unspeakable and ultimately unintelligible nature of creation. The Torah includes many names for God, referring to different aspects and definitions of manifestation. One such name is forbidden to be spoken except under certain conditions. Another one of these written names is intentionally unpronounceable (the 42-letter name), conveying an understanding that the name of God cannot be spoken, if it can even be heard by human ears.

The magic of the name, or the power of the word, is understood by many traditions to be an aspect of creative power. "*Ab'ra K'dab'ra* . . . as it reads and sounds . . . literally [translates] as 'I create what I speak.'" Furthermore, the link between chanting and the breath reveals a deeper aspect of this creative, expressive power. "One of the most ancient Hebrew words for soul is '*Neshamah,*' which literally translates as 'breath'. The Essential Self, therefore . . . is the breath of the Primary Cause."[37]

This can be applied in many ways. The Buddhist practice of *Tonglen* consciously engages the breath. *Tong* means 'giving or sending', and *len* means 'receiving or taking.' Pema Chödrön explains, "If we know of a child who is being hurt, we breathe in with the wish to take away all of that child's pain and fear. Then, as we breathe out, we send happiness, joy, or whatever would relieve the child." This is the core of the practice: breathing in others' pain so they can be well and have more space to relax and open—breathing out, sending them relaxation or whatever we feel would bring them relief and happiness.

In general, the inhale is a moment of receiving, of drawing in the information of the moment. This information may include the sounds of the world around us, our own feelings or the emotions of those with whom we are empathically connected. It can include any and all environmental factors we allow ourselves to consciously engage.

The still point or turning point of the breath is the moment at which the inhale is suspended before reversing direction. This moment can be held and extended. Drukmo Gyal, the great mantra singer and practitioner of Tibetan medicine, teaches that in our daily lives, unaware of the breath, we often neglect this critical moment. Proportionally, we spend much more time on the inhale and exhale. Thus, when meditating, great healing can be accessed by suspending the breath and allowing ourselves to integrate the energies in a moment of intentional stillness. The sophisticated system of *pranayama* (yoga of the breath or 'control of prana') engages these phases of breath in varying proportions designed to achieve different results, such as lowering or increasing the heart rate or balancing the left and right hemispheres and their corresponding impact on mental states.

The exhale is a moment of release. One can consciously release negative energies that are stuck in the body, or send positive thoughts and energies to others (*Metta*). It is a moment of giving—whether giving back or giving up in the sense of letting go.

These principles are connected with tension and resolution. The key point is that, through conscious intention, the otherwise automatic process of breathing (which happens autonomically while you sleep) becomes a mindful practice. A person reciting mantra may thus incorporate these phases of the breath as a means of engaging more actively with the energies of the moment, understanding what is being received and sent, whether intuitively or abstractly, concretely or rationally.

The mystery behind the breath is the force of creation which gives rise to it in the first place. The bellows of the universe, through its vibratory nature, pumps the breath and all other circulatory, magnetic and electrical forces at work within us. It is not intended for you to *control* the world, but to gain some discipline with the mechanism of breath, which can be used to great benefit in moments of need: physical or emotional distress, to regulate the systems of the body, invoke archetypes, or unblock obstacles to naturally flowing healing energies.

17

THE VOICE: OUR FIRST INSTRUMENT

The baby screams all day without becoming hoarse.
This is perfect harmony.

— *Lao Tzu, (Tao Te Ching)*

The first instrument is the voice. We carry it with us everywhere, and because of that, we are never without music. In many respects the voice is like any other instrument. It can be used to sing melodies, rhythms and provide musical texture. However, it differs in one critical aspect: a musical instrument is external, while the voice is internal.

Whereas a guitar, flute, drum or other instrument can be seen with the eyes, the mechanisms controlling the voice cannot be seen except through diagrams and images. When I teach guitar, I can point to a part of the instrument or move a person's hand to visibly demonstrate necessary adjustments. While it is possible to indicate various regions involved in a vocal process (such as diaphragms, vocal chords, etc.), I cannot make a person engage those things physically from within. For this reason, vocal teachers often use metaphors and other mental indicators to describe an internal process, such as visualizing singing to a person 100 feet away in order to encourage the voice to project over a greater distance.

Since the voice is connected to the physical body, it is useful to study the anatomy of the voice, as well as dietary considerations associated with the vocal tract and respiratory system. In general, warmth loosens the vocal cords while cold tightens them. Achieving homeostasis with the environment results from a well-acclimated system. Dehydration can inhibit the voice. At the same time, certain postures can constrict breathing and the windpipe, while others may improve resonance, projection, and lung capacity.

Have you ever stopped to consider what muscles control the volume of your voice? What muscles control pitch and tone? How does one imbue the voice with authentic emotion? Mastering the voice is effectively a yogic practice. Yoga means union and therefore a yogic use of the voice is to unify oneself with the divine through speech, prayer or song (written word and thought can also fall under this category). A student gains flexibility and control over the breath, diaphragms and other anatomical components involved in the process, while dealing with mental and emotional postures related to self-expression.

I often tell students that learning guitar involves 'yoga of the fingers' to improve flexibility, dexterity and precision. At first, we aren't used to putting our hands in unfamiliar postures. Even basic techniques seem foreign and impossible, but after a while the hand learns to contort itself in new ways and establish muscle memory. Likewise, the yoga of the voice brings us in touch with our bodies from the inside. The shruti box and harmonium are excellent instruments to use in conjunction with developing one's voice. They are designed like a bellows or the human lung. It helps us to see how a cycle of contraction and expansion moves air from the abdomen through the vocal tract.

Breath control is essential to singing and speaking. There are various types of breathing, such as:

1. Shallow Breathing
2. Chest Breathing
3. Abdominal Breathing

Inhalation and exhalation occur through the nose and/or mouth. There are four phases of breath:

1. Inhale
2. Full Turning Point
3. Exhale
4. Empty Turning Point

The esophagus is one of the first parts of the human body to form in utero (four to eight weeks after conception), and for this reason it carries imprints from our early development. In some traditions, the throat chakra is associated with communication and self-expression. Blockages to authentic self-expression can 'close' this chakra, resulting in timidity around using the voice, whether to speak our hearts or sing without fear and shame. Conversely, it can be 'too open,' lacking discipline and finesse, resulting in abrasive or frivolous misuse. From the perspective of sound healing, any work done to liberate and refine creative self-expression brings balance to this chakra.

Sighing, yawning, laughing and crying are four natural sound-producing processes that the body performs on its own. They are effortless. Let's take a moment to connect with our voice through them.

> 1. Sit, stand or lie flat with good, natural posture. Relax the shoulders, neck, face and head. Take a slow deep breath in through the nose. Sigh out loud, "Ahhhhh." Repeat this three or more times. Notice how you feel.

> 2. Take another breath and yawn out loud, "Ahhhh." Notice how the sigh starts more in the throat and chest and falls down, whereas the yawn starts over the top of the head. It's a

higher octave sound. Both are falling sweeps with a decompressing, oxygenating effect. Psychologically, they occur when we let our guard down and feel trusting and safe.

3. Lastly, place your hands over your heart (left hand underneath) and repeat, "Ha. Ha. Haaaa." Experiment with longer or shorter, louder or softer expressions. If laughter begins naturally, follow the wisdom of the body. Feel the resonance of the sound in your chest. 'Ha' is a heart mantra. Feel this pulsating jolt of sound, like a defibrillator stimulating the thyroid with energy and radiating out.

'Ahh' and 'Haa' are sounds which require minimal manipulation of facial muscles (compared to 'ooh,' 'eee,' and 'eye,' for instance). They are open and relaxed. The jaw hangs. Eventually, speaking and singing become as effortless and natural as these, but not before a person fully relinquishes inhibition and gets in touch with their own body enough to allow sound to pass freely from the lower abdomen, through the heart, up to the throat and from the face without constriction. When the heart is tight, vibration is choked off in the chest and sound in general comes from a shallower place. It is possible to sing from the gut, from the heart, from the throat and so on, depending on how open the central channel is from the root.

All of the chakras vibrate along this central column of energy (*sushumna*). The vagus nerve is the longest nerve in the human body. It is intimately connected with the digestive tract, heart and lungs. In fact, it extends from the colon to the brain. Speaking or singing naturally stimulates this nerve; thus, when the voice is used with awareness and control of its vibrational potency, one can bring healing to the organ systems through a form of sonic massage.

What the voice can express is endless. Our choices impact the world within and around us. Therefore, it is important to infuse one's voice with love, truth, beauty, peace and compassion.

The heart of a person cannot be left out of the voice. They are as inseparable as wisdom and truth. Therefore love, in the most profound sense of one's experience, must necessarily inform the power of the voice. To be in touch with one's heart is to align oneself with the truth of the heart. Wisdom blooms in the heart. The mind includes the heart. They are only known as separate by name. As the left cannot exist without the right, the heart cannot exist without the mind. So say what is true for both. Who knows what is true for both, but love who remembers us all? Be one with love, to be one with all—and sing, lovers, for the gift of Life. Once and for all is the victory of Peace, which cannot come but through the heart. Love knows no defeat, and each is free to do so.

Soy libre, soy bueno, y puedo querer.
I am free, I am good, and I am able to love.

—Atahualpa Yupanqui, The One Who Comes
from Far Away with Something to Say
("Soy Libre")

18

INTENSITY

Intensity is the amount of energy a sound has over an area. The same sound is more intense if you hear it in a smaller area.

— *Center for Nondestructive Evaluation,
Iowa State University*[38]

Intensity is a function of sound and music that involves a sophisticated control of various mechanisms of expression. The depth of one's life experience empowers a person to express themselves in certain areas of expertise. The sensitivity and technique of a musician or public speaker enables them to command attention, attract a listener, inspire confidence or produce a range of other emotional and psychological effects.

Intensity is not inherently good or bad. It is subjective in terms of a listener's sensitivity and mental disposition. Intensity is an axis of sound which describes a perceiver's experience of the sense impressions they receive. Sound is physically measurable in terms of wavelength and amplitude, but we are discussing intensity as it relates to emotion, psychological effect and artistry.

Greater intensity does not mean louder. It is not necessary to shout in order to inspire or teach someone. Great intensity can exist in a soft-spoken person. Learning to manipulate intensity is a subtle art that taps into one's core convictions, projected through various energetic centers (i.e., chakras) such as the heart (love), solar plexus (willpower), root (instinct, fear, survival), or throat (self-expression), etc. The projection of sound from various energetic centers can be expanded or contracted in terms of *presence*.

Some people have a dominating presence. As soon as they enter a room, even before speaking, they are *felt*. They command attention through personal magnetism. There is an *intensity* to their energy, reflected in their manner (posture and means of communicating)—a testament to their capacity to engage people with their field of consciousness. Others remain almost invisible, whether by choice or by a lack of self-confidence or effective communication skills. Boredom, distraction, incoherence and laziness also affect intensity.

Sometimes words must be loud (to project and fill space) and intense, like in the case of a public speaker who needs to address an audience of hundreds or thousands of people, sometimes without electronic amplification. At other moments, they are quietly captivating, as in the case of an actor portraying the intense fear of a person who whispers in hiding. Perhaps you want to be received in a gentle, less intense way, as when speaking to a child or in the presence of a sleeping baby. A professor may project loudly to a full auditorium while maintaining a light, friendly presence, without coming across as too intense.

These examples highlight some of the energetic properties of sound that may be projected with varying degrees of intensity. It's not what you say, but how you say it. Intensity is modified through the balance of many sonic elements, including tone, volume, speed, texture and other factors. Strong or prolonged tension may also produce high intensity through stimulation of the nervous system.

When speaking, singing or playing an instrument, see if you can express something with varying degrees of intensity:

High volume, High intensity
High volume, Low intensity
Low volume, High intensity
Low volume, Low intensity

When you mean what you say, people sense authenticity and conviction. Hesitation reduces or interrupts intensity (like a temporary signal loss), or creates a sense of the speaker's timidity, discomfort or doubt. Communicate with fervor, faith, and confidence and the intensity of what you share will be heightened.

If you don't have confidence in yourself,
it's difficult for others to have confidence in you.

— *Maestro Manuel Rufino*

In music, as you master an instrument and gain confidence in your capacity to express yourself, you will have more access to adjusting intensity, passionately and effortlessly.

Intensity can only be met by deep relaxation.
A relaxed person can go through a lot of intensity.
Intensify your postures. Intensify your meditation.
Intensify your exercises.

— *Maestro Manuel Rufino*

To reduce intensity, disengage your core. To increase it, powerfully know and trust what you are expressing, and project it with every cell of your being. Invoke it completely in thought, word and action. Practice what you preach. Walk the talk.

It is also possible to *listen* intensely (to listen intently, with intention). Focus enhances intensity. A laser is more intense than a flashlight. A magnifying glass focuses light. Reduce distraction, and you will become more acutely aware of the subject you want to observe. Remove obstacles and unwanted noise, you will gain clarity. Greater intensity comes with distinction. When something is intensely flavored with spice, it is distinctly spicy.

Intensity imbues sound with more or less gravity, density or emphasis. An intense light can be blinding, and an intense sound can be deafening. Overexposure to intense forces desensitizes us over time, overstimulating the senses and preventing them from recovering. This is 'too much of a good thing.' A sensitive person naturally experiences the world intensely, able to detect its subtleties.

19

The Elements

Traditions from around the world recognize the importance of four (and in some cases five or more) elements. These frequently include earth, air, fire and water. In some traditions, the elements space, ether, metal and or/wood may be included. The four elements are associated with the four directions (north, south, east and west), the four times of day (morning, midday, afternoon, night) as well as the four phases of life (childhood, adolescence, adulthood and old age). The 'fifth element' element is the Spirit (beyond the Earthly plane). Archangels and other etheric beings may also be invoked. These associations vary by tradition, often including regional deities or mineral, plant and animal totems—but the essence remains the same.

Each of us is composed of these fundamental forms of matter. Our bodies, which are largely composed of water, are nourished by the Earth. The air we breathe is essential to life, since it oxygenates our brain and cells. The heart pumps heat throughout the system and is often associated with fire, family, love and warmth.

In each of us, the proportions and characteristics of these elements vary. Excess and deficient wind and heat are central principles of many medical systems (notably throughout Asia), where hot and cold elements are used to treat a range of conditions, especially related to inflammation and stagnation." For instance, some people are highly rational and intellectual. They may be prone to headaches, obsessive thinking, light-headedness, distraction, overtalking or difficulties falling asleep due to an overactive mind. This points to a pronounced presence of the air element. A person like this can benefit from 'grounding,' which, as the term implies, can be achieved by connecting with the body and earth to integrate oneself with the surrounding world. Sit down, take a few deep breaths in and out through the nose, and consciously scan the body internally from head to toe. Feel whatever sensations are present. Visualize the earth beneath you, the trees, the birds or any natural images that come to mind.

This is only one basic example of how to identify and engage with an element to bring more balance to the system. Another case could be a person who is highly emotional, with limited willpower or low self-esteem. They may benefit from practicing meditation with a candle—engaging fire which is drying, illuminating and energizing. Wind can intensify fire, hence certain pranayamas and exercises that powerfully engage the breath to activate a person's 'inner fire.' Excessive grieving and volatile emotional states can be treated with water therapy such as cold showers, drinking clean water to purify toxins, bathing in rivers or oceans, etc.

Each element has many personalities, suggesting diverse applications. Water is extremely expressive. It can appear as a mystical fog, gentle rain, torrential downpour, placid lake, rushing river, stolid glacier, tidal wave and so on. Every form of water reflects a different way to connect with the power of that element. Fire can smolder, spark, rage, flicker or burn steadily. Air comes as a gentle breeze, biting wind, sudden gust or fierce tornado. The earth can form a mountain, desert, mudslide or cavern. Each manifestation expresses the various aspects of an element.

In global traditions, spirits take various forms or avatars. In the case of the feminine archetype we see it expressed as Guadalupe, Mother Mary, Tonantzin, the Green Tara, Quan Yin, Isis, Inanna, Demeter, Hecate, Kali and so on, each reflecting the nurturing, compassionate or wrathful expressions of the feminine essence. All of the elements shapeshift in this way and project different attributes.

What does this have to do with sound vibration? For one, various instruments express the elements themselves. Wind instruments (for obvious reasons) are associated with the air element. Drums and percussion beat like a heart (fire, heat). Many instruments are made of wood, metal, animal skins, intestines, seeds and gourds (earth). Rainsticks and water drums evoke the water element. Therefore the elements can be engaged through the materials used to craft the instruments themselves, and by visualizing their origins and natural environments.

Lower, guttural sounds resonate in the lower parts of the body, while bright, high pitches tend to stimulate the upper regions or chakras. However, these frequencies are not relegated to one part of the body, and I hesitate to assert any ultimate associations. Vibrations contact the entire being at once. It is not the case that a drumbeat only vibrates in the heart without reaching the rest of the body. Still, there are strong connections between certain instruments, elements, chakras and specific parts of human anatomy and cognition.

There have been various attempts to map musical scales, specific instruments and certain syllables onto the chakra and organ systems. For instance, many associate the C Major scale with other septile structures (patterns based on seven) such as the colors of the rainbow, days of the week, the seven directions (east, south, west, north, above, below, center), facial orifices (two eyes, two ears, two nostrils, mouth), chakras and planets.

The 12 note *chromatic scale* has been associated with hours on a clock, months of the year, structures in geometry ('base 60 mathematics') and the signs of the zodiac. While meaningful insights can come from these associations, meaning is often created arbitrarily, without substantial evidence, and more importantly without a personal understanding of how and why these associations came to be.

Efforts to correlate pure musical sounds with intellectual human concepts can stifle the ineffable power of sound when taken too literally. If one becomes rigid in thinking that a certain pitch must be used with a specific mantra or instrument in order to heal a certain part of the body, then the art of sound healing is reduced to dogmatic and mechanical principles.

Very often man gives great importance to color and tone—so much so that he forgets that which is behind them, and that leads into many superstitions, fancies and imaginations. Many people have fooled the simple ones by telling them what color belonged to their souls, or what note belonged to their lives.

— Hazrat Inayat Khan
(The Mystery of Color and Sound)

We are exploring the relationship between impermanent *form* and eternal *essence*. In music, there are many forms. It may appear that classical arias, blues, indigenous chants and country music have little to do with one another, but understanding the elements of melody, harmony and rhythm reveal that music is a universal language easily understood and translated when you know what to listen for.

In general, 12 musical pitches are used (although other scales and tuning systems do exist, elaborated later in this book). These 12 notes compose the chromatic scale (from Greek 'khroma,' meaning 'color'). The overwhelming majority of music made in the world is essentially composed of these 12 sonic colors (not including genres such as noise music or other avant-garde streams). Certain instruments and vocal traditions use microtones (smaller intervals that require a great deal of sensitivity as a listener to identify) but the basic 12 are widely used. Much of the time, only 7 or even 5 of these are chosen for a composition (a reduced collection of notes is also known as a key, scale or mode). This means that millions of songs heard around the world are composed of very few unique notes. It's like painting: the primary colors number three, but an infinite array of hues can be created from them. Similarly, the ingredients in bread are simple, yet every culture has a distinct way of preparing it.

The *essence* of musical elements, such as pitch and rhythm, apply to any *form* given to a melody, mantra, harmony, etc. Since 12 fundamental pitches are used to compose most music in the world, a major distinguishing factor from one style to the next is the rhythmic profile of the genre. Reggae music uses characteristic rhythms (listen especially to rhythm guitar strumming patterns). Jazz is often identified with a 'swing' feel, which tends to emphasize beats two and four (also known as the 'backbeat') and includes many unexpected syncopations ('upbeats' or 'offbeats'). Country music has a very particular language of melodic fragments, canonic chord progressions and traditional rhythms.

Fluency in any language requires familiarity with its vocabulary, inflections, syntax and pacing of speech. You can say the right words in another language, but a native speaker might not understand you if your rhythmic delivery is irregular. They grew up hearing certain cultural cadences, and you come speaking with your own cadences. One must master this nuance of language in order to achieve clear, effective communication.

Becoming fluent in a musical style requires assimilating not only melodic and harmonic paradigms (structures widely used in the genre), but also rhythmic gestures, common forms, traditional instrumentation and thematic content (i.e. lyric subject matter, source texts in the case of mantra recitation, and traditional songs inherited culturally through direct aural transmission). In many musical traditions, when a specific song should be played is dependent on the time of day, season, religious function, etc. Therefore learning a musical tradition (such as Indian *raga* or indigenous chanting) may require knowledge of an entire cosmological system.

One effective way to learn language is to immerse oneself in it completely. Go to the culture directly. Live like a local.

Seek the company of masters and traditional people. Engage in conversation. Thanks to recorded music, we have a veritable Alexandrian library of music at our fingertips. It is possible to expose oneself to music from around the world and throughout history.

Understanding the following musical principles will enable you to more efficiently identify the characteristic aspects of any genre or piece of music: What instruments are being used? What scales or modes (collections of notes taken from the basic 12) are generating the melodies? What time signatures and tempos are most common to the style? Is the music harmonically busy or centered around monotone drones and chanting?

In music there is a concept known as text-painting, referring to the way in which a composer portrays a literary image through sound. Can you strum a guitar to emulate a roaring fire, or play cascading arpeggios on the piano to imitate a waterfall? Can your drum embody the flapping wings of an eagle? This requires imagination, creativity, intention and a way of listening to nature to converse fluently in its many languages.

In general, water is a healing tonic. Drinking clean water flushes the system of toxins (processed principally through the liver) and promotes healthy cells. The blood, excretory fluids, brain fluids and other chemicals are also associated with the 'waters' of the body. The endocrine system deals with regulation of hormones and chemicals which are transported via bodily fluids. These glands are responsible for the release of dopamine, melatonin, oxytocin, testosterone, estrogen and so forth, which are connected with procreation, dream states, hallucination and a wide spectrum of emotions.

The moon is also associated with water due to its connection with the tides and the 28 day menstrual cycle. For this reason the water element is often associated with emotions, the womb, desires and so on. The pineal gland performs many functions pertaining to this system and is involved with interdependent communication between the brain, organs and other systems.

Tiny crystals (earth element) have been found to play a role in this.[39]

> . . . *biomineralization has been studied in the pineal gland of the human brain. It consists of small crystals that are less than 20 microm in length and that are completely distinct from the often observed mulberry-type hydroxyapatite concretions. A special procedure was developed for isolation of the crystals from the organic matter in the pineal gland. Cubic, hexagonal, and cylindrical morphologies have been identified using scanning electron microscopy.*
>
> — *National Library of Medicine*

The pineal gland is sometimes referred to as the 'third eye' due to its involvement with internal visionary states. Often symbolized by a pinecone, it appears throughout esoteric symbols dating back to at least ancient Sumeria, and has been of significance to ancient medical systems that are foundational to modern science.[40]

The modern Rx medical symbol has ancient roots dating back to at least the Eye of Horus in ancient Egypt.

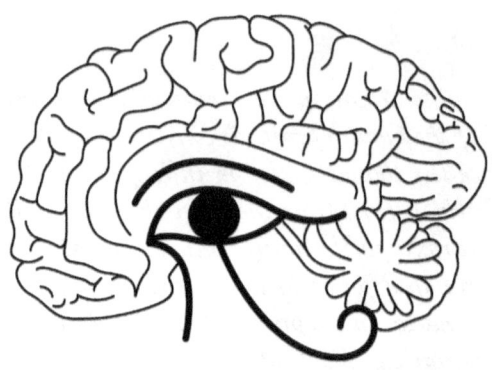

Commonly referred to as the 'third eye,' the pineal gland is associated with one's inner capacity for visualization and the regulation of the endocrine system.

Various pathways and means of communication exist between all parts of the body. For this reason, the elements should be understood as interdependent. The excess of one implies imbalance with the others. Sound therapy can promote balance as readily as it can disrupt it when used improperly.

As a medical doctor decides which scalpel to use, a sound healer must know which instruments to use in the course of meditation. Guided meditation is a form of psychotherapy designed to help a person identify and transform malignant thoughtforms. However, it is not enough to simply cut a person open and remove a tumor. The doctor must also seal the wound, nourish the body back to health and advise the patient in lifestyle choices to prevent recurrence. Likewise, a sound healer is involved in a holistic process of assessment and treatment.

The following teaching is paraphrased from Maestro Manuel Rufino:

Air: When you're born, you take your first breath. If the air element is not activated properly, the doctor needs to attach you to a breathalyzer. You may suffer problems with the lungs and respiratory system throughout life.

Fire: When the breath is active, the heart is able to beat. Without a strong pulse and if body heat is low, they need to place you in an incubator. A person who requires this may experience problems with sensitivity to hot and cold temperatures.

Water: When the heart is functioning well, it pumps blood and other fluids throughout the body. If these fluids are not flowing, they need to connect you to an IV. Such a person may have problems with the circulatory system.

Earth: Finally, the doctor tests your muscle response by checking if you are able to grip their finger in your hand. If the baby exhibits low response in the physical body, it is possible they will suffer bone, nail and hair problems.

This elemental process is a microcosm of the medicine wheel described at the outset of this chapter. Complete healing takes into account a complex series of mental, emotional and physical factors. What modern science calls genetic predisposition, ancient Vedic science calls karma—the principles of action, cause and effect. Sound therapy is able to address all of these contributing factors and can be used as a complementary modality in conjunction with internal and external therapies.

PART II

MUSIC THEORY: LITERACY OF THE LANGUAGE

Part II

NOTE TO THE READER

The following chapters are intended for musicians and non-musicians alike. While it may seem foreign and technical at times, try to connect with the content however you can. Trained musicians are encouraged to revisit these essential principles of music theory. Only with a strong, core understanding can more subtle and sophisticated systems of analysis emerge.

A house is not built from the roof down. The stronger your foundation, the better supported and expansive your freedom of expression can be. Do not take pedagogical information for granted, or at face value. Meditate deeply on why these principles have come to be standardized and disseminated for thousands of years. If you sing or play an instrument, apply these concepts for yourself to experience them sonically.

This is not a music theory method book. If you are interested in practicing and developing an expanded knowledge of these principles, you are encouraged to pursue additional study, whether through a teacher or the myriad resources available in printed, recorded and digitally distributed forms. The more senses you involve in the learning process, the more holistically you can integrate sound and music with your body, mind and spirit.

Music theory can be articulated in many ways. The system I am presenting is derived largely from what may be called 'Western, European classical and jazz theory,' and assumes the use of a 12-tone equal temperament tuning system. This was the basis of my musical training. However, it is my belief that music is a universal form of communication. These theoretical principles have allowed me to integrate music from around the world. It is not my intention to exclude the perspectives of other theoretical traditions (as in India or the Middle East where they have their own sophisticated systems and terminology), nor am I suggesting that this system is all-encompassing. Rather, I am choosing to speak in my 'native language.'

Like language itself, music theory is constantly adapting. Attaining basic fluency with this theoretical system and learning to apply it will enable you to converse much more easily with global musical traditions of all kinds.

I

The Language of Music

Music theory is an ancient discipline, a science and philosophy that bridges worlds between language, physics, mathematics and cosmology. While many point to Pythagoras of ancient Greece as an early exponent of music theory, it is clear that the Egyptians, Hindus, Arabs and many Native peoples around the world have also made significant contributions to our understanding of how to organize and implement sound with intention.

I have spoken with many individuals who feel that studying music theory would box them in, limit their creativity or somehow stifle their unique voice. For those who hold that perspective, I compare music to language. Although we don't *require* written language in order to speak, it is clear that reading and writing are deeply beneficial skills that enrich learning and self-expression.

Music theory is, in essence, the alphabet, grammar and syntax of music. The 12 pitches (notes) of the chromatic scale are one such alphabet. How these notes are combined to create harmony is musical spelling and vocabulary. Stringing notes together to make coherent melodies is akin to formatting words into sentence structures. There are exclamations, questions, monologues, dialogues and other interactions epitomized by musical choices.

The study of rhythm relates to punctuation in language. Long and short pauses, space, silence and syllabic count contribute to our sense of flow and timing. In poetry, rhythm is studied deeply and applied to form through rhyme and meter (such as iambic pentameter in Shakespearean sonnets, or the strict formal considerations of the haiku, villanelle, sestina, etc.). Poets even use sonic elements such as alliteration, rhyme and metaphor which blur the lines between music and language and emphasize patterns and harmony.

Of course, written language could never fully capture one's speaking style, just as written music cannot notate every intricacy and subtlety of musical expression. No recording technology has been able to capture or reproduce the full presence of a live performance. There is always something in spirit or essence which evades our attempts at documentation, lost in translation from the vibrating present to the page or disk.

Although formal training in music theory and performance technique are not prerequisite to becoming an extraordinary or virtuosic artist (much less a healer or meditation guide), it has been my experience that submitting oneself to this discipline will open doors to understanding, collaborating and generally unlocking self-expression in profound ways.

Knowing what notes belong to a key allows you to determine what key an instrument or song is in. Knowing what notes belong to a chord allows you to choose instruments that harmonize well together. Practicing ear training (also known as 'aural skills') will dramatically improve call and response, as well as your ability to translate the music you hear inside through an instrument. Understanding rhythm, meter and form speeds up the process of learning melodies and memorizing songs, as patterns emerge. All of this enhances one's capacity for emulation, composition and improvisation.

It is not necessary to read in order to cook, but if you can read, you can follow recipes on your own to learn techniques and properties of ingredients. You can experiment in ways that are inaccessible to an illiterate person. When a person teaches you a song, it's like the proverbial 'giving a man a fish.' When you can teach yourself a song, you have learned to fish. There is no more dependence on others to show you a new trick, teach you a new chord, or tell you whether or not an instrument will work in a given context. You can hear and determine for yourself what is harmonious.

Musical analysis is not meant to take the magic or mystery out of music. It is not intended to over-intellectualize the experience or convert you into a technocrat. It is not for you to feel superior to others because they lack certain knowledge and it is certainly not meant to establish any dogmas about 'right' or 'wrong' notes or musical aesthetics.

Music theory has nothing to do with your subjective perception of beauty. It makes no claims about supremacy or inferiority in artistry. It is a neutral tool, just as atomic energy can be harnessed for both creation and destruction.

Neither is music theory an opinion. On certain levels, it deals with very measurable relationships including ratios (expressed as intervals, or the distance from one note to another), volume (measured in decibels), and frequencies (pitches measured in hertz). It makes use of advanced knowledge in physics and geometry to develop instruments, concert halls, recording technology and tuning systems that are constantly evolving as new considerations are taken into account.

It is beyond the scope of this book to teach you the ins and outs of music theory, much less the sophisticated physics of vibration and instrument design; rather, it is to inspire you towards that exploration for yourself, wherever the journey leads you. Each subject is introduced as a doorway—it's up to you to enter and explore the world within. There are countless resources on the internet, in books, academic institutions and approaches to practicing independently that will help you unshroud these mysteries and reveal the elegant, coherent tapestry of how sounds interact and relate with the universe.

As with learning any language, music is best assimilated through immersion. Have musical conversations, practice alone and with others, listen critically and apply all you have learned so that you find yourself speaking the language. One day, if you are disciplined enough to achieve it, these principles will become cohesive and contextualized.

With regards to light and color theory, computers employ a hexadecimal system. While this remains a limited array, it is vastly more expressive than 8 bit color, for instance. Likewise, the 12 pitches of this standard musical system must be understood as a useful orientation—but only to a point. Beyond a certain level, the organic processor of human consciousness refuses to confine itself to such limited terms. The infinite gradients and subtleties between sounds (sometimes referred to as 'microtones') cannot be articulated in the 12 pitches of the chromatic scale. Likewise, rhythm is more fluid than metronomic. In reality, musical expression is infinite, depending on the sensitivity and precision of the perceiver.

This is not to say that limited theoretical systems are wrong, nor are they inherently stifling just because they are partial. On the contrary, organizational logic is useful for contextualizing many things. You have to learn the rules before you can break them consciously. How can you renounce something you don't possess? How can you discredit something you have not mastered? Eventually, any theoretical framework must be transcended to access a fuller picture, but not before you are able to make sense of and utilize it. Otherwise, it is an arbitrary rejection of something you do not yet understand.

The purpose of studying and applying music theory is to perfect technique, allowing the individual to achieve greater dominion over their ability to express themselves. Total expressive fluency with sound is defined as the ability to produce any frequency (high or low) of any timbre (tonal quality) at any time (speed or duration) and volume level (loud or soft).

2

Notes

A musical note, also known as a pitch, is defined by the frequency at which it vibrates. We measure sonic frequency in hertz (Hz). Today, one of the most common *tuning systems* in the world is based on the standard: A = 440 Hz. This means that the pitch 'A' (above 'middle C') produces 440 vibrations per second. If it vibrates slower than that, it goes *flat*, or lowers until it becomes another pitch. If it vibrates faster, it goes *sharp*, or raises until it becomes a higher pitch. Graphically, a frequency can be represented as a sine wave:

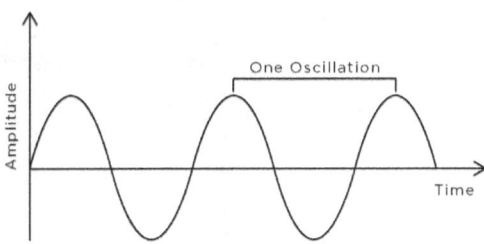

Any tuning system involves a human-determined logic for calculating the distance from one note to another (known as an interval). For example, *just intonation* uses whole number ratios in an attempt to construct 'mathematically perfect' intervals (such as an octave which is 2:1). We can visualize a string that is twice as long as another. It will sound 'one octave' lower. In mathematical terms, A 440 Hz vibrates twice as fast as A 220 Hz, one octave lower. The limitation of this tuning system is that some combinations of notes produce whole number ratios, while others do not (especially if we attempt to change keys).

Therefore *equal temperament* was devised to split the octave evenly into 12 half-steps. In equal temperament, the distance between notes is determined logarithmically rather than by whole number ratios. There are distinct sonic differences between these systems, with the latter being more flexible when combining all 12 of the commonly used 'half-steps' or 'semi-tones.' Other tuning systems exist, but these two should provide some context for understanding that tuning logic is variable.

There have been various tuning systems throughout history and around the world. Today, the international standard is based on A 440 Hz (an agreement establishing this tuning standard was signed in 1953 and is maintained by the International Standards Organization), but many musicians, especially those interested in sound healing, are beginning to experiment with A 432 Hz more frequently. There are many reasons for this, since the number 432 is related to various astronomical aspects of our solar system and organic phenomena in our world (such as geometric proportions). For this reason, some consider it to be a more 'harmonious' frequency in terms of its sympathetic resonance with nature, although this is a matter of debate.

Extensive examples of these theories can be found through many sources. Several commonly cited examples include: the width of the moon is approximately 2,160 miles (432 x 5). The orbital precession of the equinoxes takes 25,920 years (divided by 2,160 = 12, divided by 432 = 60). 108, a number employed in ancient malas and mandalas, as well as various Native American ceremonies, is a subdivision of 432. 432/6 = 72, a significant and sacred number in many traditions, such as the 72 names of God in Judaism. 4+3+2 = 9, a symbol of significance in numerology. 432/12 = 36, pertaining to the trinity in Christian numerology, and the 36 righteous Tzadikim in Kabbalah. There are 43,200 seconds in 12 hours. We breathe in and out approximately 21,600 times in one day (432 x 50). 432/3 = 144: "And they sang a new song before the throne and before the four living creatures and the elders. No one could learn the song except the 144,000 who had been redeemed from the earth." Rev.

14:1-3. The cross-relationships between these numbers play heavily into base 60 mathematics and thus geometry and the platonic solids (triangle = 180°, tetrahedron = 720°, square = 320°, cube = 2160°, octahedron = 1440°). The above examples only scratch the surface of this field of study, sufficient to inspire further research. Of course, the mathematical standards used to support these examples are enforced by humans and are not universal (metric, imperial and standard measurement provide different results, for instance). Therefore, one must be cautious when ascribing cosmological significance to culturally subjective measurements.

While there are good reasons to consider A 432 Hz, it is important to remember that much recorded music has been tuned to A 440 Hz, music which touches people's hearts deeply and can help unlock memories in those with age-related dementia and Alzheimers.[41] Thus, to suggest that A 440 Hz is *not* a healing frequency ignores the immense volume of touching artistry produced in the modern world, and the mounting evidence of its tangible benefits in music therapy.

No matter what tuning system is chosen, the stability of any frequency is fundamental to our capacity to recognize it. If a pitch fluctuates erratically, it sounds random and chaotic. The same is true for visible vibrations. Colors vibrate within distinct frequency ranges measured in nanometers, which is why we are able to identify them as red, blue and so on. If the frequency changes, the color changes and vice versa.

In music, when a note is vibrating at a reliable, chosen frequency, we say that it is 'in tune.' Intonation refers to the accuracy or precision of a note, whether sung or played on an instrument. A note can be in tune or out of tune unto itself, as well as in context with other notes. A guitar, for instance, has six strings. All of these need to be in tune with each other in order for the instrument to work as it was designed to. Some instruments cannot be re-tuned, such as harmonicas, hand pans, electric pianos and certain types of traditional flutes. These are tuned by the manufacturer and cannot be modified later. Thus, a guitar or other instrument with tuning mechanisms is flexible and can match an instrument with fixed tuning. In many cases, playing in 432 is not even an option unless the instrument itself was designed that way.

Typically, people use external tuners or tune by ear to match a given pitch. Some people are able to hear a pitch internally without needing to check it with another. A person who can readily identify a note by name upon hearing it is said to have *perfect pitch*. This may seem like an incredible skill, but it's no more incredible than a person who can recognize the color red upon seeing it, or identify the shape of various geometric structures (cone, cylinder, cube, hexagon, etc.) or differentiate the taste of garlic from the taste of onion. It is possible to train the ear to recognize various pitches. This is the work of ear training, also known as aural skills.

Although perfect pitch may seem desirable, it can have unwanted side-effects. A person with perfect pitch might be bothered by any music that is even slightly 'out of tune.' Their ears expect music to occur in a certain format that is by no means the only correct or necessary way. Rather, tuning standards such as A 440 Hz are arbitrary, and have changed throughout history as the music world experimented with different instruments and tuning systems such as equal temperament, just intonation, meantone temperament, etc. Nonetheless, if a person has perfect pitch and is able to appreciate the color of alternate tunings, this skill can be an asset for rapidly learning and analyzing music.

Even if one never develops perfect pitch (which is certainly not necessary in order to become an extraordinary artist, healer or musician) it is of great benefit to improve *relative pitch*. Relative pitch refers to one's ability to recognize a note in context with others. If someone plays a note on a piano for instance, I may not recognize the pitch unless I am told what it is. But once told, I can orient myself by it to identify subsequent pitches, like using the Northern Star to orient oneself to the cardinal directions. Once you learn which star is the Northern Star, you can use that knowledge to identify other stars and constellations in relation to it.

In music, each note has a specific frequency measured in hertz. Worldwide, humanity often emphasizes 12 primary notes (although microtones are also found throughout the world). From these 12, melodic and harmonic material is derived. Every melody and chord is simply a permutation or combination of these 12 (just as the 26 letters of the English alphabet create every word in the dictionary and every work of literature in the English language). This does not include certain expressive elements such as pitch bending, vibrato and the use of micro-tones. The 12 standard pitches in this system comprise the chromatic scale. These are:

1. C
2. C#/Db[†]
3. D
4. D#/Eb
5. E[†]
6. F
7. F#/Gb
8. G
9. G#/Ab
10. A
11. A#/Bb
12. B

# = sharp
b = flat

[†] C# sounds the same as Db, but it is 'spelled' differently. This is known as an 'enharmonic equivalent'.

[†] You may notice that there is no E#/Fb or B#/Cb written here. That is part of a deeper conversation in music theory beyond the scope of this introduction.

After B, we return to C again. This cycle repeats infinitely in lower and higher octaves. In general we use #'s when ascending and b's when descending the chromatic scale. These 12 pitches can also be visualized using a clock:

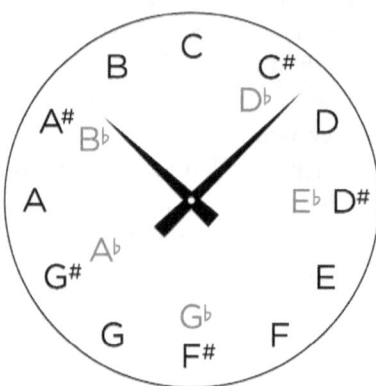

In reality, it's more of a spiral than a circle, since we are always moving up or down into higher and lower octaves (faster and slower frequencies). Spatially, sound moves through more dimensions than a two-dimensional clock-face can allow us to perceive.

In the chromatic scale, the distance from each note to the next is called a half-step, also known as a minor 2nd. This is an example of an *interval*.

3

INTERVALS

An interval simply means *the distance from one note to another*.

An octave is an example of an interval. An octave expresses a 2:1 ratio (A 440 Hz is one octave below A 880 Hz, which vibrates twice as fast). Each interval has a fixed distance with a particular sonic signature that the ear can learn to identify as readily as the color red or the shape of a triangle. Because there are 12 notes in the common musical system, there are 12 unique intervals within an octave (the octave marking the beginning of the cycle in a higher or lower range):

1. Unison	(no distance)	i.e. C to C	0 half-steps
2. Half-Step	(minor 2nd)	C to Db	1 half-step
3. Whole-Step	(Major 2nd)	C to D	2 half-steps
4. Minor Third	(Augmented 2nd)	C to Eb	3 half-steps
5. Major Third		C to E	4 half-steps
6. Perfect 4th		C to F	5 half-steps
7. Tritone	(half an octave)	C to F#/Gb	6 half-steps
8. Perfect 5th		C to G	7 half-steps
9. Minor 6th	(Augmented 5th)	C to Ab	8 half-steps
10. Major 6th		C to A	9 half-steps
11. Minor 7th		C to Bb	10 half-steps
12. Major 7th		C to B	11 half-steps
13/1. Octave		C to C	12 half-steps

Just as one yard has a fixed definition of 36 inches, and a foot has a fixed definition of 12 inches, each interval is constructed with its own fixed distance of half-steps. For instance, a unison always means 'two of the same note', with no distance from one note to the other. An example of this would be two people singing the same melody at the same time.

A half-step is the smallest unit of measurement used in this system of music theory, although microtones smaller than a half-step are also found throughout the world.

Since this system uses twelve notes separated by half-steps, let us say that each half-step is 'one inch' apart. Here is a miniature of a 12" ruler, not drawn to scale:

0	1	2	3	4	5	6	7	8	9	10	11	(12)
C	C#/Db	D	D#/Eb	E	F	F#/Gb	G	G#/Ab	A	A#/Bb	B	(C)

Another name for a half-step is a 'minor 2nd'. The distance from any note to another note one half-step away is an example of a minor 2nd. A Major 2nd is separated by two half-steps (two 'inches'). A minor 3rd is separated by three half-steps (three 'inches'). A Major 3rd is separated by four half-steps (four 'inches) and so on.

An interval can be built on any starting note (also known as a *root* or *fundamental*), not only C. Thus a whole step above D is E, because D to D# is one half-step (minor 2nd) and D to E is two half-steps (known as a whole step or Major 2nd).

D	(D#)	E
0	(1)	2

If we count from C up to B (without using sharps and flats), we reach 7:

C	D	E	F	G	A	B	(C)
1	2	3	4	5	6	7	(8/1)

We can also count in reverse order, from C *down* to B for a distance of 2. Here is the same content in reverse:

C	B	A	G	F	E	D	(C)
1	2	3	4	5	6	7	(8/1)

It is possible to count up *or* down from any note. Picture a ladder with eight rungs:

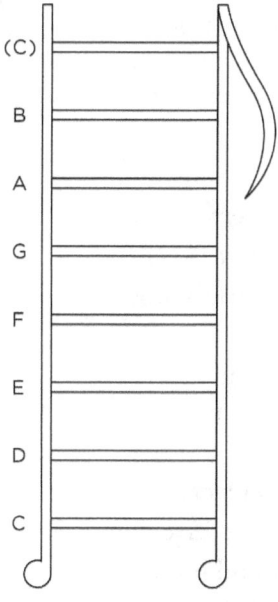

The third rung up from the bottom is also the sixth rung down from the top. Upon closer analysis, this reveals an interesting pattern:

C to C	(stay on 1, or down 8)	1 + 8 = 9
C to D	(up 2, or down 7)	2 + 7 = 9
C to E	(up 3, or down 6)	3 + 6 = 9
C to F	(up 4, or down 5)	4 + 5 = 9
C to G	(up 5, or down 4)	5 + 4 = 9
C to A	(up 6, or down 3)	6 + 3 = 9
C to B	(up 7, or down 2)	7 + 2 = 9
C to C	(up 8, or stay on 1)	8 + 1 = 9

What does this reveal? It demonstrates the principle of *inversion*. An inversion refers to the displacement of notes belonging to a musical structure into higher or lower octaves. In this case, we are inverting intervals (such as C *below* E, versus C *above* E). We can extrapolate the following:

» Unison inverts to Octave
» 2nds invert to 7ths
» 3rds invert to 6ths
» 4ths invert to 5ths

When applied to the chromatic scale (twelve notes instead of only seven) there are more specific insights:

» Unison inverts to Octave
» minor 2nd inverts to Major 7th
» Major 2nd inverts to minor 7th
» minor 3rd inverts to Major 6th

» Major 3rd inverts to minor 6th
» Perfect 4th inverts to Perfect 5th
» Tritone inverts to Tritone (octave split in half)

This information is useful because it creates shortcuts and simplifies the process of memorizing intervals and their relationships to one another, revealing patterns and pathways between structures. These inversions are like positive and negative exposures in photography. There is always a latent aspect waiting to be revealed. Just as night completes day by providing contrast, inversions provide a fuller picture of how one interval relates to its complement. As above, so below. Again the principle of correspondence expresses itself through sound.

In brief, intervals are fixed distances. They each have a unique sound which can be memorized and readily recognized. Beyond an octave, intervals essentially repeat, but in a spread (expanded) form. For simplicity, we generally condense intervals within an octave to analyze them more efficiently.

4

SCALES:
MAJOR, MINOR AND OTHER MODES

A scale is a collection of pitches that follow a specific pattern of intervals, typically involving whole-steps (W) and half-steps (H), although microtones and other relationships can exist. A scale in any octave range (high or low) expresses a key. A *key* or *key signature* tells us which of the 12 fundamental pitches are being included or omitted. The Major scale has the following structure:

W   W   H   W   W   W   H

C (W) D (W) E (H) F (W) G (W) A (W) B (H) C

This is one of the most common musical scales in the world. You might know it from the "Sound of Music," where Julie Andrews teaches a group of children music theory through song to memorize: Do—Re—Mi—Fa—So—La—Ti/Si—(Do), a vocal system of music education known as solfege. This seven-note scale provides the underlying architecture for literally millions of compositions. In Europe, the syllables chosen for the scale have been in use for 1,000 years. Guido D'Arezzo is the Italian music theorist credited with the codification of this system. Originally, "Do" was "Ut", and the entire series was based on the *"Ut Queant Laxis"* or "Hymn to St. John the Baptist":

Ut queant laxīs
*Re*sonāre fibrīs
*Mī*ra gestōrum
*Fa*mulī tuōrum,
*So*lve pollūtī
*La*biī reātum,
*Sā*ncte *I*ohannēs.

It translates as: "So that your servants may, with loosened voices, resound the wonders of your deeds, clean the guilt from our stained lips, O Saint John."

Whatever associations may exist with regards to the Christian church, this scale is not exclusive to Europe, and genres as seemingly disparate as bossa nova and Hindustani ragas make use of it. In regions of India, the same scale is sung with different syllables:

Sa Re Ga Ma Pa Dha Ni

The minor scale follows the same pattern, but starting on the 6th note of the scale instead of the 1st. This preserves the order of the notes but offsets them, like rotating a clock so that 12 starts in the 9 position. The sequence of notes remains the same, but they are introduced from a different starting point:

MAJOR

C	D	E	F	G	(A)	B
1	2	3	4	5	(6)	7
Do	Re	Mi	Fa	So	La	Si
W	W	H	W	W	(W)	H

MINOR

(A)	B	C	D	E	F	G
(1)	2	3	4	5	6	7
(La)	Si	Do	Re	Mi	Fa	So
(W)	H	W	W	H	W	W

The pattern of intervals used to construct the Major/minor scale is *asymmetrical*. Other types of scales, such as the 'chromatic', 'diminished' (also known as 'octatonic') and 'whole tone' scales are *symmetrical*:

Chromatic: H H H H H H H H H H H H
(12 Notes)

Diminished: W H W H W H W H
(8 Notes, hence   or
the term 'octatonic')   H W H W H W H W

Whole Tone: W W W W W W
(6 Notes)

Certain scales use wider interval skips, such as thirds. The Pentatonic scale is a five note scale that can be seen as a reduction of the diatonic Major/minor scale:

Major Pentatonic: W W m3 W m3
(5 Notes)

minor Pentatonic: m3 W W m3 W
(5 Notes)

Here is a side-by-side comparison of the Major and pentatonic scale:

Major Scale: C D E F G A B
                1 2 3 4 5 6 7

Pentatonic Scale: C D E G A
                   1 2 3 4 5

Major, minor and other Modes

While the teachings of music theory go into much greater subtlety and detail, one essential distinction to understand is the relationship between *Major* and *minor*. These are two sides of the same coin, dark and light. They are, in fact, inversions of each other. Major is typically (although not necessarily) associated with happier, lighter, more joyful sounds. Minor, by contrast, tends to be more introspective, melancholic and dark.

Interestingly, these two personalities are drawn from an identical collection of notes and are therefore *modes* of one another. The C Major scale, as an example, is made up of the following seven notes, which repeat infinitely in lower and higher octaves:

C   D   E   F   G   A   B   (C)

The minor scale uses the exact same notes, but starting on A instead of C:

A   B   C   D   E   F   G   (A)

The significant difference in sound between these two, despite their nearly identical structure, is created by *emphasis*. When the note C is introduced first and emphasized throughout a piece of music, the listener processes the music as a composition in the C Major mode (also known as the key of C Major). If, by contrast, the note A is first introduced and emphasized, the listener will perceive the music in the A minor mode.

In language, context is essential to our comprehension of meaning. Consider the following homonyms (words that sound the same but are spelled differently and have different meanings):

Their   There   They're

The context in which these words appear determines their function. Without context, the mind cannot decide which spelling is appropriate.

Modality refers to this process of orientation within a collection of pitches. Because there are seven notes in this scale, there are also seven modes, whose names derive from Greek:

1	Ionian	starting on C	(Major)
2	Dorian	starting on D	
3	Phrygian	starting on E	
4	Lydian	starting on F	
5	Mixolydian	starting on G	
6	Aeolian	starting on A	(relative minor)
7	Locrian	starting on B	

Modes work like a combination lock. The first mode would begin with scale degrees 1, 2, 3, the second mode would begin with scale degrees 2, 3, 4, and so on:

1st mode: 1 2 3 4 5 6 7   (1)

2nd mode: 2 3 4 5 6 7 1   (2)

3rd mode: 3 4 5 6 7 1 2   (3)

etc.

    Each mode has a distinct sound, even though it is constructed using the same seven notes. This is because emphasis is placed on different parts of the scale. The C Major scale has seven notes, thus it has seven modes:

Mode 1:	C	D	E	F	G	A	B	(C)
	1	2	3	4	5	6	7	(1)

Mode 2:	D	E	F	G	A	B	C	(D)
	2	3	4	5	6	7	1	(2)

Mode 3:	E	F	G	A	B	C	C	(E)
	3	4	5	6	7	1	2	(3)

Mode 4:	F	G	A	B	C	D	E	(F)
	4	5	6	7	1	2	3	(4)

Mode 5:	G	A	B	C	D	E	F	(G)
	5	6	7	1	2	3	4	(5)

Mode 6:	A	B	C	D	E	F	G	(A)
	6	7	1	2	3	4	5	(6)

Mode 7:	B	C	D	E	F	G	A	(B)
	7	1	2	3	4	5	6	(7)

Music from around the world uses various forms of scales and modes, but these underlying mechanics are universal:

1. A scale, key or mode is built on a fundamental pitch or 'root.'

2. A series of intervals is chosen in relation to that pitch, which constitute the scale or mode.

3. These notes can be shuffled and reordered freely to create variations in emphasis.

Another important aspect of the musical scale is the principle of the octave. Octaves, as the name implies, refer to the 8th note in the scale, which in the case of C Major brings us back to 1, the original starting pitch. That is to say: C in the higher 'octave'.

C	D	E	F	G	A	B	(C)
1	2	3	4	5	6	7	(8/1) 'octave'

This pattern repeats infinitely in lower and higher octaves. If you can visualize a piano keyboard, you will notice that there are 12 notes (7 white and 5 black). After the 12th note, we arrive at the original position in the next octave, which then repeats the same pattern. The white keys are the seven notes of the C Major scale.

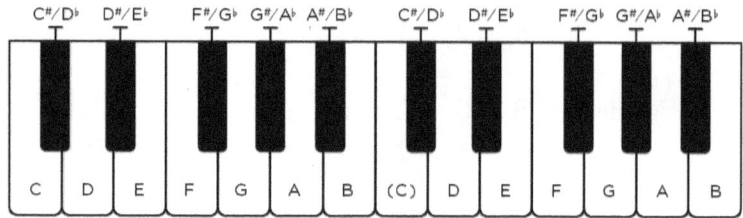

Two octaves on a piano keyboard.

Although the human ear can only hear within a limited range, pitches do repeat in lower and higher octaves. High and low, like sound and silence, express a polarity of sound.

Any note can occur in high and low octaves. These stimulate us differently since their waveforms have different physical properties. Thus the pitch 'C' is not an absolute structure. Different expressions of 'C' in terms of tone, volume, timbre (color of sound), octave and instrumentation can drastically vary the character and thus the impact of its sound. Context is critical. To suggest that producing a certain tone always has the same effect is an oversimplification, due to various sonic properties and how they interact with consciousness.

Voicing Ranges

Traditionally, choral music (vocal music for a choir) is divided into four vocal ranges. From high to low these are:

(S) Soprano
(A) Alto
(T) Tenor
(B) Bass

Men generally have lower speaking voices and thus lower singing ranges as well. Typically, men sing in the tenor and bass range. Women, having higher pitched voices, often occupy the alto and soprano range. This is not fixed. There are many singers of both genders whose voices may fall in the opposite category, or who have broad vocal ranges that extend even from bass up to soprano.

In general, there is a comfortable, natural range for a person's voice. This can be expanded and strengthened in weaker areas through vocal training and engagement of lesser-used muscle groups. The mechanics of the voice are contained within our physical bodies. Tone, pitch and volume are controlled by muscles, diaphragms, moisture and breath—which can be regulated and developed like any muscle or bodily system. Diet, breath exercises, physical disciplines and simple mental shifts can be practiced to enhance the capacity of the vocal system. While it is necessary to explore this for oneself, practical training with an experienced teacher can be invaluable to better understand and gain access to these controls.

Using the voice requires technique like any instrument. While a flute has holes, reeds and a method of tuning which are located *externally* on the instrument itself, the voice has equivalent mechanisms that must be explored *internally*. Like a car with switches and pedals for speed, power, air and electronics—the voice has various mechanisms to manipulate dynamics (loud and quiet), pitch (high and low), tone (harsh or gentle) and a range of other effects.

5

TRIADS, CHORDS, ARPEGGIOS
AND OTHER STRUCTURES

Like intervals, a triad (three notes played simultaneously) is one
type of structure in music which adheres to a particular formula.
If an interval refers to the distance from point A to point B, a
triad connects them to point C, introducing a third dimension.
Triads are a type of chord made by stacking three notes (each
separated by an interval of a third) on top of one another and
played simultaneously. There are four types of triads:

Major

minor

diminished

Augmented

Each of these triads has a particular compositional structure.
Just as a square is defined by four equal sides, each triad adheres
to its own laws. The formulas of the four basic triads are:

1. MAJOR TRIAD = Major 3rd above starting note,
   then a minor 3rd above that

Note names:	C	E	G
Number of half-steps:	0	4	7

C to E is a Major 3rd, E to G is a minor 3rd.

2. MINOR TRIAD = minor 3rd above starting note,
   then a Major 3rd above that

Note names:	C	Eb	G
Number of half-steps:	0	3	7

C to Eb is a minor 3rd, Eb to G is a Major 3rd.

3. DIMINISHED TRIAD = minor 3rd above starting
   then a minor 3rd above that

Note names:	C	Eb	Gb
Number of half-steps:	0	3	6

C to Eb is a minor 3rd, Eb to Gb is another minor 3rd

4. AUGMENTED TRIAD = Major 3rd above starting note,
   then a Major 3rd above that

Note names:	C	E	G#
Number of half-steps:	0	4	8

C to E is a Major 3rd, E to G# is another Major 3rd

The above examples are given with the root note C, although a triad can be built on any of the 12 chromatic pitches, also known as 'fundamentals' or 'roots'.

You may notice some patterns here. For one, the structure of Major and minor triads are inverted. While a Major triad is constructed with a Major 3rd on the bottom and a minor 3rd on top, a minor triad is just the opposite; minor 3rd on the bottom, Major 3rd on top. Inversions are an important aspect of music as they reveal deeper relationships between apparently different structures. The Major and minor modes share the same notes, but they are inversions of one another:

CDEFGAB

ABCDEFG

The remaining two triads are *symmetrical*. Diminished triads are composed of two minor 3rds, and Augmented triads are composed of two Major 3rds. These are much less common, especially the Augmented triad.

As previously discussed, chords are *vertical* structures created by stacking notes on top of each other, whereas melodies are a series of individual notes coming one after another. Chords lay a foundation over which melodies are played. They are also called *harmonies* because they refer to the harmonization of multiple notes together with a melody.

Triads are examples of three-note chordal structures. *All triads are chords, but not all chords are triads.* Some chords contain more than three notes, as in the case of 7th Chords which extend the pattern by stacking another 3rd on top.

Triads:	1	3	5	
7th chords:	1	3	5	7
	C	E	G	B

Other harmonic structures exist which do not adhere to the principle of stacking 3rds. These could be composed of any combination of intervals, such as 2nds or 4ths. Broadly speaking, trichords are three note structures, tetrachords are four note structures, followed by pentachords, hexachords, etc. These can be extremely complex and are generally the subject of advanced theory beyond the scope of this book.

For now, let us say that a chord refers to any structure in which three or more notes are played simultaneously to create a harmony.

A chord can also be split apart, stratified and outlined one note at a time as an *arpeggio*. Imagine a child building a tower with three blocks. A chord is represented by those blocks stacked vertically, and an arpeggio is represented by them next to each other on the floor. The same three 'blocks' or notes belong to the chord. The difference is that an arpeggio introduces them sequentially rather than simultaneously.

G (5)
E (3)
C (1)   vs   CEG (135)

Chords are introduced in a sequence to create *chord progressions*. Many songs follow simple chord progressions that use three or four chords in a repeating loop. This is a bit like DNA. We label the building blocks of DNA: ACTG. Let's take A, C and G since these are *actually* chords in music. We can make six variations from those letters, each of which might constitute a chord progression in a song:

A C G
A G C
C A G
C G A
G A C
G C A

As more chord types are introduced and linked together, the options increase exponentially. If each chord is a neuron in the musical brain, chord progressions are the associations we make between them to create context and function. They are the building blocks of song forms and structures. The same principle applies to single-note melodies, which are supported by these underlying harmonies.

The fact that different terms and symbols can be used to describe similar things in music can be a source of confusion. There are different theoretical languages to describe music throughout the world and even within one musical culture. The important thing is to develop a functional musical vocabulary, so you can begin to identify and describe distinct aspects of music, especially notes and rhythms which are the foundations of all musical structures, including melodies, chords and compositional forms.

6

Voice-Leading and Resolution: Tritones and Leading Tones

If you play a 'wrong note,'
you're only a half-step away from the 'right' one.
— Unknown

After a 'mono-tone' melody (remaining on a single pitch-center), there is an inevitable choice: up or down? As soon as a second note is introduced (higher or lower than the starting pitch) an interval is created. When enough of these pitches are introduced, a melodic and harmonic context is implied. We call this the key or mode of the song.

As we begin to select notes, weighted and separated by intervals and rhythmic emphasis, tendencies emerge which cause the ear to expect resolution. These implied resolutions are perhaps the result of cultural programming in which we have grown accustomed to melodic, harmonic and rhythmic gestures, just as we are accustomed to patterns of speech, familiar greetings, etc.

Throughout life, whether you're conscious of it or not, you have heard various musical gestures thousands of times. The same resolutions occur in genres as seemingly disparate as classical music and hip-hop. Nonetheless, their unifying aspects are undeniable. Whether these tendencies result from subjective taste or are inherent to the human ear, emerging from the sonic geometry of nature, they inform our musical aesthetics.

It has been my observation that many animals in nature make use of certain intervals in their calls and songs, especially the 'Perfect 5th' (ratio 3/2). Coqui frogs, morning doves and chickens, for instance, often produce this interval. The 5th *resolving* to the Root (or 'tonic') is a 'returning home' motion in music. The *tonic* is the fundamental note which feels like home, where the music is centered, arrives, or resolves.

It is also worth noting that the *Pentatonic* (five tone) scale is almost ubiquitously used as the underpinning structure in the music of indigenous and traditional people throughout the world, from Buddhist mantras to African songs, indigenous *icaros* (sacred incantations) and chants throughout the Americas. The same is true for folk music across Europe as well as aboriginal Australian music. I have yet to find a culture which does not employ this particular scale in its traditional music.

There is already extensive information available on what is called the *overtone series*. In brief, the overtone series is a natural harmonic series of *sympathetically resonant* pitches that occur whenever a single note is played. To understand this, consider a prism. When we look at the sun, we tend to perceive it as a single color. Once filtered through a prism, sunlight divides into a spectrum of colors. Likewise, a fundamental pitch can be parsed into overtones and undertones. In general, these overtones sequentially decrease in volume while the intervals between them grow smaller:

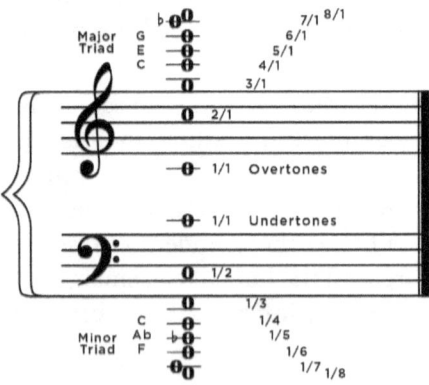

The overtone series phenomenon teaches us that a 'single' pitch is in fact composed of multiple frequencies which are mathematically related. When we break a note apart and emphasize these overtones, we can hear this series of related tones more clearly.

The overtone series is characterized by certain ratios that closely relate to the pentatonic scale (having 4 of 5 notes in common). This reveals a basis in sound physics to support a natural tendency in human musical culture. If you'd like to learn more about the overtone series, read George Russel's *Lydian Chromatic Concept of Tonal Organization*, or simply explore the vast resources available online.

Listen to Mongolian throat singing for a clear demonstration of this phenomenon executed with precise control. Through such vocal techniques we know that the human voice is capable of producing multiple notes at once.

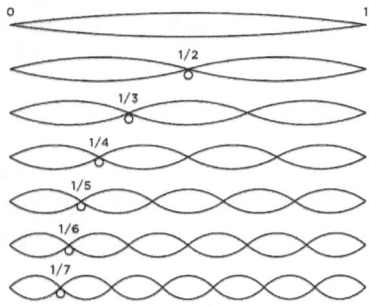

The seven note scale, by contrast, introduces two notes which are very particular in their potency. Let's compare the Pentatonic (five note) and Diatonic (seven note) scales. Notice that one is contained within the other:

Pentatonic:	C	D	E		G	A	
Diatonic:	C	D	E	(F)	G	A	(B)
	1	2	3	(4)	5	6	(7)

In the key of C, the two notes that are added to the Pentatonic scale are the 4th and 7th scale degrees. Together, these construct an interval called a *tritone* (splitting the octave in half). What makes these notes particularly potent is their strong tendencies to resolve. These notes have a sonic magnetism that implies an expected resolution. In general, scale degree 4 resolves *down* to 3, while scale degree 7 resolves *up* to 1. The 7th scale degree is also called the *leading tone* because it *leads* the ear to resolve to the root or 'tonic' of the established home key. This contrary motion further enhances the sense of resolution.

Any note can resolve up *or* down, but natural tendency often suggests the direction of its resolution. Choosing to move in contrary motion creates an unexpected departure by default, if only because we have grown accustomed to hearing certain resolutions more commonly for hundreds or thousands of years.

The tritone unto itself is a potent interval. For one, the two notes are 6 half-steps apart, essentially splitting the octave down the middle (remember there are 12 pitches). If the octave is harmonious, splitting it in half naturally results in a vibration that sounds far away.

One of the most common harmonic motions in music is the 'Dominant-Tonic' resolution (also referred to as a 'V-I' relationship). In the key of C, this would involve the Major triads G and C, or the chord 'G7' resolving to a C Major triad. Let's look at their structures:

G7:	G	B	D	F
C:	C	E	G	

Now let's rearrange them to see the closest motion of their resolutions:

G7:	G	B	F	D
C:	G	C	E	

When moving from one chord to the next, the most logical voice-leading is the path of least resistance, or the smallest motion necessary to resolve from one note to another. In this case, B is very close to C, and F is very close to E. The most efficient voice-leading makes use of these pathways.

F down to	E
D down to	C or up to E
B up to	C
G remain on	G

The main thing to understand is that chords are clusters of individual notes. Rather than moving from one chord to another, it is important to see that a collection of individual notes is following a series of pathways, or *resolutions*, into the next harmony. The harmonies are vertical structures, but the melodic pathways are horizontal. These two dimensions are inseparable.

Notes can move in three ways relative to each other:

1. Contrary motion:
   > two notes move in opposite directions

2. Parallel motion:
   > two notes move in a similar direction

3. Oblique motion:
   > one note remains stationary while
   > the other moves up or down

7

Rhythm

*Everything flows, out and in; everything has its tides;
all things rise and fall; the pendulum-swing manifests
in everything; the measure of the swing to the right is the
measure of the swing to the left; rhythm Compensates.*

— *Three Initiates (The Kybalion)*

Rhythm expresses the relationship between sound and time. Musical time, like time itself, exists within a unified continuum. Only once you apply a system of measurement does time divide into units. In everyday life, these are years, months, weeks, days, hours, seconds and so on. In musical language, these are movements, sections, measures, bars, beats, subdivisions, and other such terms.

The basic pulse of music is the *beat*. Like a heartbeat, this is a reliable undercurrent or pattern amidst the ebbs and flows of melody; the ups and downs of dynamic drama. Musical phrases generally fit into groups of beats called *measures* (or 'bars') which are counted using *time-signatures*. One prevalent time-signature is 4/4 or 'common time.' This 4/4 time refers to a sequence of four beats, evenly spaced and of equal value. Because four beats divide one measure, they are called *quarter notes*. In relation to this, we can derive various commonly used rhythmic values:

Whole Note	=	4 beats
Half Note	=	2 beats
Quarter Note	=	1 beat
Eighth Note	=	1/2 beat
Sixteenth Note	=	1/4 beat
etc.		

The relationship between each is 2:1. A whole note lasts twice as long as a half note. A half note lasts twice as long as a quarter note, and so on. The relationship of a whole note to the others is as follows:

Whole Note	=	1:1
Half Note	=	2:1
Quarter Note	=	4:1
Eighth Note	=	8:1
Sixteenth Note	=	16:1
Etc.		

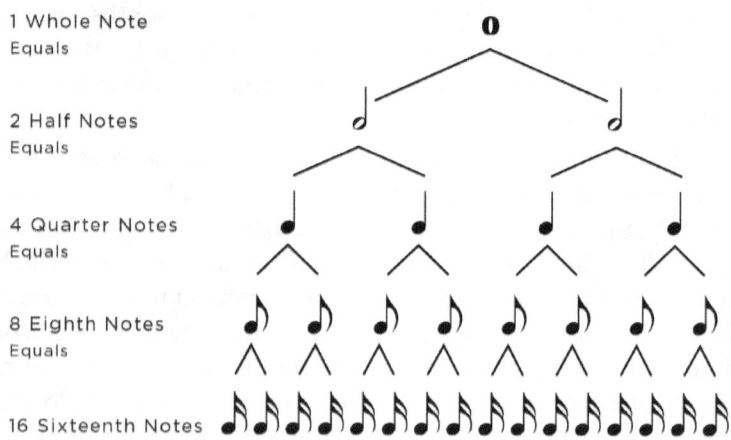

1 Whole Note
Equals

2 Half Notes
Equals

4 Quarter Notes
Equals

8 Eighth Notes
Equals

16 Sixteenth Notes

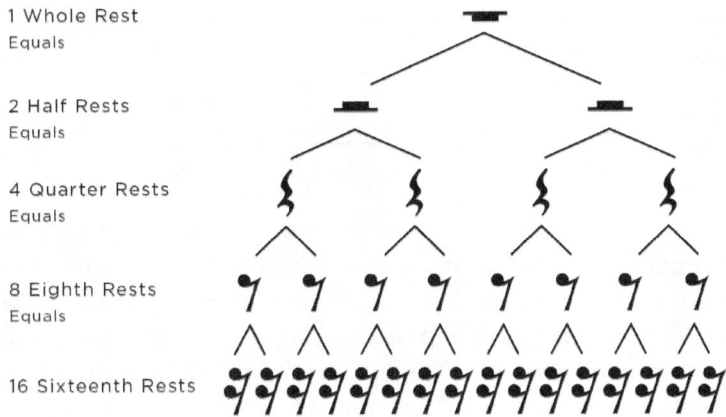

1 Whole Rest
Equals

2 Half Rests
Equals

4 Quarter Rests
Equals

8 Eighth Rests
Equals

16 Sixteenth Rests

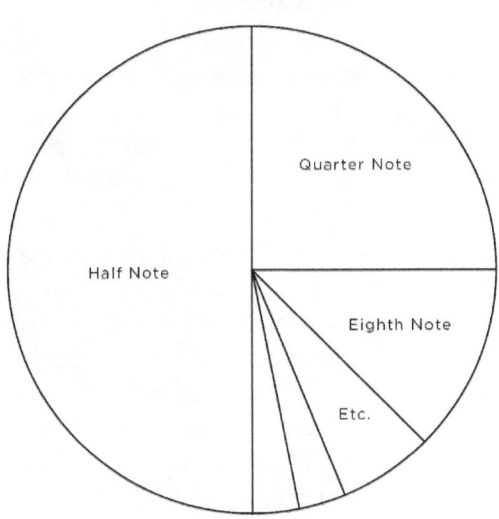

Whole Note

Quarter Note

Half Note

Eighth Note

Etc.

Let's assume the tempo (speed) of a song is 60 beats per minute, or *BPMs*. This means that, like the second hand on a clock, the underlying pulse of the music beats 60 times per minute. In 4/4 time (if we divide 60 by four) we get 15 measures. 15 measures with four beats each = 60 beats in one minute. The length of these notes is determined by basic division and ratios.

Whole Note or Whole Rest (4 beats)							
Half Note (2 beats)				Half Note (2 beats)			
Quarter Note (1 beat)		Quarter Note (1 beat)		Quarter Note (1 beat)		Quarter Note (1 beat)	
Eighth Note (1/2 beat)	Eighth Note (1/2 beat)	Eighth Note (1/2 beat)	Eighth Note (1/2 beat)	Eighth Note (1/2 beat)	Eighth Note (1/2 beat)	Eighth Note (1/2 beat)	Eighth Note (1/2 beat)
etc.							

In this example of 60 beats per minute, four beats (i.e. four seconds) is the duration of one *whole-note*. Two beats (two seconds) is a *half note*. One beat (one second) is a *quarter note*. An eighth-note equals half of a second, a sixteenth-note equals a quarter of a second, and so on. There is one whole-note lasting four beats in a measure of 4/4 time. There can be two half-notes per measure, four quarter-notes, eight eighth-notes, or sixteen sixteenth-notes, in the same timespan.

This highlights the basic relationship between different rhythmic values. Just as we measure a day in hours, half hours and other useful segments of time, we can develop a functional sense of how long things last in music, whether counting entire sections and song forms, a few measures or smaller units within them.

It is important to make a distinction between a time signature and the tempo at which it is played. For instance, one measure of 4/4 time played at 60 BPM would last four seconds, but one measure of 4/4 time played at 120 BPM (twice as fast, the approximate speed of a human heartbeat) would last only two seconds. Thus, tempo is independent of meter (also known as time signature). In the raga traditions of India, these terms are related to what is known as a 'tala cycle'.

Although no written rhythmic system is needed to make music, rhythm theory *can* be used to analyze music that is made without it. Time goes on, whether you measure it by a clock or not. Colors radiate, whether you label them or not. Music theory offers a Rosetta Stone through which we can interpret the music of other cultures.

Four corners epitomize the framework of a square, just as four beats establish the framework of a measure in 4/4 time. Three corners form the structure of a triangle, just as three beats form a measure of 3/4 time. As the name implies, 3/4 is a time signature in which one measure contains three quarter notes.

The two main categories of time signatures are *even meter* and *odd meter*, with even meter (especially 4/4) being by far the most common in 'popular' music. A few examples of different meters are:

Even Meter	Odd Meter
4/4	7/4
2/4	5/4
12/8	3/4
	6/8[†]

You may have noticed that time-signatures in this system are expressed as fractions. Fractions, when related to each other, have common denominators. These common denominators reveal the cross-relationships between different meters.

$$4/4 \times 3 = 12 \text{ beats}$$

$$3/4 \times 4 = 12 \text{ beats}$$

Thus, three measures of 4/4 time contain the same number of beats as four measures of 3/4 time. Both equal 12 beats. When these two are imposed on top of each other, the result is called a *polyrhythm*. A polyrhythm is like two divergent roads that arrive at the same point in the end: Beat 1. They are not parallel roads, rather one may be seen as a straight line (the shortest way from point A to point B) while the other may take a more circuitous route.

There are many types of polyrhythms. The relationship between 3 and 4 is one of the simpler ones to grasp. In general, musical cultures of the Indian subcontinent and throughout

(† It is worth noting that other time signatures and combinations can exist, producing complex groupings such as 18/8 or the use of decimals, as well as frequent changes between different time signatures within a piece of music.)

Africa and the Middle East are masters of rhythmic elements, including another important musical element: subdivision.

One way to approach subdivision is to compare the following fractions:

$$3/4 \times 2 = 6/8$$

3/4 and 6/8 last the same amount of time, but these time signatures have different feelings. One measure of 3/4 emphasizes three quarter notes per measure. One measure of 6/8 emphasizes six eighth-notes per measure. As we learned earlier, the relationship between quarter-notes and eighth-notes is 2:1. That is the essential relationship between 3/4 and 6/8 as well. 6/8 may feel 'twice as fast', but in reality it simply emphasizes eight notes instead of the quarter notes, which have a longer duration or '*value*'.

If it weren't for *emphasis*, we wouldn't experience any differentiation between one beat and the next. If it weren't for the minute and hour hands on a clock, the seconds would click by indefinitely without any broader periodic intervals to orient ourselves by. In music, this emphasis occurs on *strong* and *weak* beats, or as downbeats and upbeats.

In the case of 4/4 time, the strong beats are: one and three. The weak beats are: two and four. Different genres achieve their distinct identity partly through rhythmic emphasis. A 'shuffle' rhythm emphasizes beats one and three, whereas a 'swing' beat emphasizes two and four. Much of the popular music in recent times, such as hip-hop, funk and R&B, emphasize beats two and four, also known as the 'backbeat'.

1　　2　　3　　4

1　　2　　3　　4

Furthermore, there is a smaller-scale downbeat/upbeat relationship. In one measure of 4/4, there are four quarter notes.

In the same space of time, there are eight eighth-notes. Thus eighth notes can be counted in the subdivision (pronouncing 'and' for the + sign):

$$
\begin{array}{ccccccc}
1 & & 2 & & 3 & & 4 \\
1 & + & 2 & + & 3 & + & 4
\end{array}
$$

The 'and' symbols are syncopations (aka offbeats). Rather than occurring 'on the beat,' they occur in between. These syncopations provide a lot of rhythmic personality, depending on which ones are emphasized or omitted. Jazz and latin music especially emphasize syncopation, creating a bouncy sensation, and unexpected start and end points for melodic phrases. In general, Caribbean and Latin music are heavily influenced by rhythms from Africa, since the African diaspora resulted in a melting pot of musical styles throughout the American continent.

Syncopations are spring-loaded. They are anticipatory, creating a strong sense of rhythmic drive to resolve on a strong beat. Here is a sentence to illustrate the feeling of this. Read the first sentence normally, and in the second example, emphasize the words in bold:

There is a dog in the backyard.

1	2	3	4
There **is** a	**dog** in	**the** back	**yard.**

Now try emphasizing the *opposite* side of the beat:

1	2	3	4
There is	a dog	**in** the	**back** yard.

An eight syllable sentence is used here to closely reflect the eighth-notes counted in one measure of 4/4 time:

1	2	3	4	5	6	7	8
There	is	a	dog	in	the	back	yard.

Another important aspect of rhythm and tempo to consider is how one *stretches* time. There is some flexibility regarding landing 'on the beat.' Rhythmically speaking, a note may come 'ahead of,' 'on,' or 'behind' the beat. There is a range, just as a bullseye on a dart board has some flexibility. It is larger than the point of the dart itself.

Some might say that playing ahead of the beat is 'rushing,' while playing behind the beat is 'dragging.' To play 'on the beat' more or less implies metronomic perfection (the perfectly even click of a clock's second-hand). *Rushing* creates a feeling that music is speeding up. It can feel anxious, like the music is being *pushed* or forced to go faster than is settled or natural. Playing *behind* the beat is the opposite, contributing to a sense of lethargy, as if things are heavy and slowing down, like a car running out of gas on the road gradually losing its capacity to accelerate until the whole thing drags to a halt.

The only difference between playing ahead of or behind the beat, and rushing vs. dragging, is that one is intentional while the other demonstrates a lack of consistent technique. To *intentionally* play ahead of or behind the beat does not imply that the tempo is changing. The pulse of the music neither speeds up nor slows down. Rather, it is an *affect*, like a southern drawl might sound languid, patient and slow, while a city slicker sounds fast-paced. Both are able to communicate clearly and effectively, but the energies driving their speech patterns are noticeably different.

It is also possible to intentionally slow down or speed up, whether suddenly or gradually within a song. Again, this should be a musical choice, not an unconscious habit due to one's lack of rhythmic stability. The best way to strengthen one's rhythmic foundation is to practice with a metronome (a musical tool which clicks at a consistent rate measured in Beats Per Minute; i.e., 60 beats per minute = 60 seconds).

If pitch (high and low frequency) is the vertical axis of music, rhythm (placement in time) is the horizontal axis.

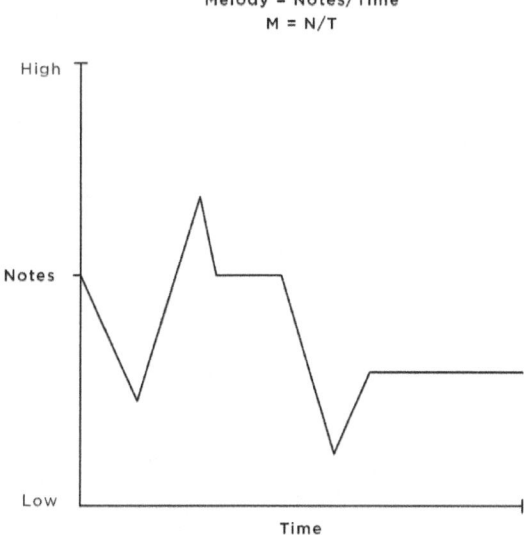

Melody = Notes/Time
M = N/T

The interaction of pitch and rhythm produces sound, illustrating our definition of a melody: Melody = Notes/Time. There is no pitch without rhythm, and no rhythm without pitch. Even percussive instruments, such as drums, produce pitch. Many drums can be tuned, and the notes they produce depend on the tightness of the skin, resonance of the wood, size of the drum, and how the instrument is struck.

All audible sounds are identified by the frequencies they produce. Even a note (let's say A440 hz) is defined by how many times a pressure wave repeats itself in one second. Therefore, rhythm is an inherent aspect of melody.

8

COMMON TONES AND MOTIVES:
UNIFYING PRINCIPLES
AND THEMATIC DEVELOPMENT

A motive is the essence of a composition, like the nucleus of an atom. It is a point of origin from which the music can unfold to become a monumental creation. From the moment of conception, an entire body is implied. Just as our DNA contains the blueprint of our entire being in every cell, so the opening phrase of a melody implies the music to come. Cultivating a motive in a clear, focused way is a process of following musical ideas through to fruition. The peak of this fruition may be harvested in a single moment such as a musical climax or gratifying resolution. It requires an enormous tree to yield even one small seed after years of growing. That single seed can produce an entire forest. If we judged the potential of a seed by its size, we would never imagine the forest it could produce.

In music, a single note, rhythm or melodic motive may be the generating seed of a symphony. This is the principle of *theme and variations*—a method of redefining musical material in different contexts to infuse it with new life. It's like taking the color blue and juxtaposing it against different backgrounds. How does blue interact with white? How does it interact with yellow, red, green, etc.? Blue is the constant and these variables lend different expressions of mood.

A *common tone* is a note that is shared by multiple scales, chords, etc. For instance, the following chords all contain a common tone, in this case the note C:

C Major :	CEG
F Major :	FAC
A minor :	ACE
D-7 :	DFAC
F#-7(b5) :	F#ACE

This common tone allows for the pitch C to be placed in different harmonic contexts, and these are only a few of many possibilities. Placing the same note in a different context is called *reharmonization*. There are 12 notes, but literally thousands of contexts they could be placed in, just as there are 26 letters but thousands of words.

A mathematical principle relevant to music is permutation. Permutation calculates how many possibilities there are for shuffling around a group of notes. Think of it this way—a restaurant has some primary ingredients (rice, beans, onions, etc.). These are recombined in different ways to create tacos, burritos, fajitas and so on. Similarly, musical permutations present the same notes in different forms.

To illustrate this point, let's construct a C Major triad:

Notes in a C Major Triad: C   E   G

Using the principle of permutation, we can produce the following variations:

C	E	G
C	G	E
E	C	G
E	G	C
G	C	E
G	E	C

These are called *inversions* of the same three notes. No matter what order they appear in, together they spell a C Major triad. This differs slightly in written language. The word 'free' can be rearranged to spell 'reef,' but these words have very different meanings. In music however, these inversions are closely related and can function in the same harmonic context regardless of their shuffled order. Nonetheless, each reordered grouping is distinct and has its own flavor or personality.

An inversion is any multi-note structure in which its notes are shuffled to produce a different order. Any inversion can be *voiced* in a higher or lower octave. Therefore *voicings* refer to the range of notes included, while the inversion is the order in which the notes appear.

Rhythmic variations can also be derived from permutations. Let's say we have four beats (one measure of 4/4 time):

$$1 \qquad 2 \qquad 3 \qquad 4$$

Say we want to *emphasize* different beats. Let's represent the emphasized beats in **bold**. Try reading the following sequences, twice each (perhaps along with a metronome, one click per number) with spoken emphasis on the bold numbers:

1	2	3	4
1	**2**	3	4
1	2	**3**	4
1	2	3	**4**
1	2	**3**	4
1	**2**	3	**4**
1	2	3	**4**
1	**2**	**3**	4
1	**2**	3	4
1	2	**3**	**4**

There are many other permutations, and as soon as we include eighth-notes instead of just quarter-notes, we double our core material, and thus exponentially increase the permutative possibilities.

Math is useful, because it systematically reveals options we might not have considered.

People speak idiomatically. The same is true in music. We tend to imitate what we are accustomed to hearing in culturally familiar music. By mapping out other solutions, we gain access to less familiar patterns. The technique of permutation can be applied to rhythmic, melodic and harmonic content.

Another way of recycling musical material is to *modulate* or *transpose* it.

Frequency Modulation

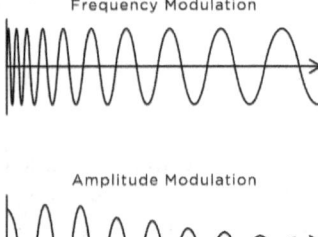

Amplitude Modulation

An interval, scale or chord can be built on any note. Usually, the starting note or opening interval (since it orients our ears to the musical context) will tell us what key we are in. The process of changing a song from one key to another is called *transposition*. Try singing the 'Happy Birthday' song. Notice what note you start on and isolate that note. Now intentionally move that note higher or lower. From this new pitch, again sing 'Happy Birthday.' What you have just done is to *transpose* the song into another key.

Transposition is useful, because we may want to sing in a range that is more suitable for our particular voice. Or we may have instruments which are only compatible with certain keys (such as a pentatonic flute or handpan). This is especially true of instruments that do not produce all 12 notes and are therefore limited to certain keys.

Similarly, *metric modulation* means to adapt a song or other musical material into a different meter or time-signature. For instance, 'Happy Birthday' is normally performed in 3/4 time, but it could be adapted to 4/4 time by prolonging notes or adding a beat to every measure. Metric modulation can also happen within a piece of music from one section to another.

Rhythmic displacement is another example of modifying a theme by starting it at different points in time, such as a 'round' where one person sings the melody and another joins slightly later with the same melody, so that the two are overlapped but offset.

These concepts can be hard to implement without a sophisticated understanding and control of rhythm. However, most of us do it intuitively when guided, without needing to understand how it works. These concepts are difficult to translate into words. It is essential to have a direct, experiential knowledge of music. A teacher can be an indispensable guide in the process. Nonetheless, knowledge of rhythm is in the body, perhaps best expressed through dance, which is rhythm made visible.

Each time we play a piece of music, it's different. The energy of the performer changes. The response of the audience changes. The venue may be different. The timbre of the instrument can change due to varying humidity or the corrosion of strings. The energy of each day is different. These changes may be subtle, but they are always present, contributing to the character of the music. Music studios attempt to mitigate these variables by establishing temperature and humidity conditions, *sound baffling* materials and mathematically precise placements of microphones and instruments.

Some artists pride themselves on reproducing nearly identical performances time after time, to give people what they expect and deliver a reliable act. When a musician develops core repertoire, they either hone a refined, consistent presentation, or intentionally change it up to keep it interesting and adapt it to various audiences and environments. For example, they may choose to play slowly and quietly when the mood is calm or the venue is intimate.

Arranging or *arrangement* refers to the process of preparing music for a given situation or a particular instrumentation—the voices and/or instruments used to perform the piece. An arrangement can be for one voice or an entire symphonic orchestra. You can sing 'Happy Birthday' solo, or you can write an elaborate score for many instruments and voices. Arrangement makes a piece adaptable. One may choose to emulate or reproduce an arrangement as precisely as possible (as in the case of cover bands) or choose to reimagine it completely. Arrangements make use of all of the elements of sound we have discussed so far and can involve a sophisticated series of expressive choices.

Arrangements can be prepared beforehand with intention, or they can be created spontaneously through a process of improvisation. Improvisation is to music what casual conversation is to speech. You don't read from a script. You draw from vocabulary and grammar to spontaneously respond in dialogue. Composition is improvisation *slowed down*, with the option to edit and revise. It takes longer to write than to speak in general, just as it takes longer to compose than to spontaneously improvise.

The more one cultivates fluency in the language of music, the more freely one can improvise. Technical proficiency and a keen awareness of musical options allow one to draw upon a vast palette of expression. A world of possibilities opens up gradually, until even a simple motive becomes a generating seed for limitless variation and expansion.

9

Genres, Styles and Traditions: Preservationist and Experimental Approaches

Considering all of the *elements of sound* and music discussed so far, we arrive at the point where these elements are consciously combined to create a work of art. This manifests in many forms: songs, chants, prayers, poems, mantras, concertos—with all of the attributes that typify a tradition. What distinguishes one style from another are its rhythmic, melodic and harmonic idioms, instruments used by the culture, and other considerations of thematic content.

When learning a piece of music, it is important to learn it as accurately as possible. Thanks to the advent of written and recorded music, it is often possible to 'go to the source,' and consult the original material. Initially, one should strive to emulate the melody (notes and rhythms) and the chords (harmonies) that were chosen to support it, *before* modifying it in other ways.

> *Once you know the rule, you can break it.*
> *But the one who knows the rule never breaks it,*
> *he transcends it.*
>
> — *Maestro Manuel Rufino*

Some artists are preservationists. They are committed to reproducing traditional music, thereby maintaining a living tradition and ensuring that it is not lost or distorted over time. Their work is of great value to musical diversity, history and ethnomusicology, helping humanity retain legacies of music. In many cases, music composed before the recording era has been transformed over the centuries, like a game of telephone in which the original transmission is intentionally or inadvertently modified.

Other artists are experimental, choosing to adapt to modern aesthetics and pioneer original styles. Such artists may deconstruct, *reharmonize* (change the chords) or reinterpret traditional music in ways that deviate significantly from their original expression—but again, in order to break a rule, you must first learn it. Otherwise, it is not a conscious decision. Loose interpretation is often the result of incomplete or inaccurate learning.

Before making something your own, strive to master the raw material. Naturally, your distinct voice will find room to express itself within the framework of extant music. This is especially true when collaborating with others. Compromise, find common ground, otherwise you might find yourself in a traditional setting unable to converse with appropriate stylistic finesse.

We may never recover the unique *affects* of previous generations, just as we gradually lose the accents and colloquialisms of different eras, regions and cultural groups. Hearing recordings of a typical American accent from 75 years ago, it is clear that we have strayed far from the speaking manner of our ancestors. The same is true of their music. The turn of the 20th century is about as far back as we can go without having to consult written descriptions of how music may have sounded, which is a far cry from actually hearing it.

Special knowledge is preserved in ancient music, like a species that continues to adapt since prehistoric times.

These unbroken vibrations maintain a connection to our ancestry which is a living link between the past and the present. Most of what we have, we owe to our ancestors. Knowledge in the modern world has been passed down from teacher to student. When atrocities occur (such genocide or cultural erasure) humanity registers a gap in knowledge, like a fragmented file wiped from a hard-drive. While nature has its necessary ways of purging and shaking up the globe (cleansing forest fires, floods, ice ages, etc.), this should not suggest that humanity benefits by destroying its own artistic and spiritual legacies.

Sometimes, ancient wisdom becomes diluted and adulterated, as in the case of religious dogma that distorts the essence of teachings its prophets intended. In other cases, our cultural inheritance is a source of great honor and value. The *Bhagavad Gita*, *Tao Te Ching*, teachings of the Buddha, *The Bible*, *Popol Vuh*, *Quran*, the poetry of Rumi, Hermetic writings, the epic poetry and philosophy of the ancient Greeks and countless other pillars of human genius have had a tremendous, formative impact on human society. They have been guides to kings and emperors as well as lay people, influencing politics, art, science, religion and beyond. We are fortunate that these teachings have been documented, translated, protected and disseminated for thousands of years. Of course they have been misappropriated to justify war and hatred, but that was not their original purpose, nor is it their predominant legacy.

Less obvious are the impacts of preserved oral teachings. In ancient times, much sacred knowledge was forbidden to be written down. Hundreds of thousands of verses were memorized verbatim by disciples. Their accuracy and consistency was preserved to an astounding degree (as in the case of the Vedas which were found in nearly identical forms among people divided by centuries and vast geographical distances). In this way, sound and music have a life of their own, which defy the narrow boundaries of a page. Before recording technology, and even still, sound cannot be completely documented, and must therefore be transmitted from mouth to ear, so to speak.

When we participate in reciting an ancient song or mantra, we are engaging in a practice that has been ongoing for countless generations. There are tribes in the Amazon who are so ancient that in some cases they no longer know the translations of their songs, and yet they continue to preserve them. Just as we value the wisdom and life experience of a teacher, we ought to acknowledge the accumulated power and energy of these transgenerational vibrations. They outlive the blinking eye of a human lifetime and serve as connective tissues between ancient and modern times. Just as a battery is charged, these vibrations are imbued with power by virtue of their perpetual activation.

Culturally, we share many lullabies and stories that serve as a unifying repertoire. They shape our worldviews, and with each generation, we reinforce or dispense with folkloric archetypes depending on the proclivities of our times.

> *Myths are public dreams,*
> *dreams are private myths.*
>
> —*Joseph Campbell*

Houses are many, home is one. Wars are many, violence is one. Lovers are many, love is one. Songs are many, music is one. Do not be deceived by the apparent differences between genres, forms and time periods. Just as skin color distracts us from recognizing our inherent, shared humanity, superficial differences in sonic aesthetics distract us from the unifying characteristics of sound and music.

IO

Practice and Discipline

Better than 100 years of idleness,
is one day spent in determination.

— *Gautama Buddha (The Dhammapada)*

Each of us learns differently. We all have strengths and weaknesses. It is important to play to our strengths and challenge ourselves to overcome limitations. Through the study of music we assimilate many things: rhythm, melody, harmony, theory, technique, expressivity and so on. There are so many factors to consider that the process can feel overwhelming. It can be easy to overlook details and difficult to understand new concepts. Without consistent practice, we can lose what ground we've gained. For this reason, I recommend developing practice strategies and sticking with them regularly, while remaining flexible and forgiving for not always meeting our own expectations.

The efficacy of practice is not determined solely by time spent. A short, focused practice routine is more effective than a long, unfocused one. Learn efficiently. One can spend hundreds of hours playing over the course of years without much improvement. However, a person who commits to developing themselves in areas that are weak can advance rapidly. Quality over quantity. Focused practice for a few minutes a day (especially before bed when the mind is prepared to integrate knowledge during rest) will yield consistent results.

Taking lessons with a qualified teacher is an excellent way to grow, especially when your will and determination can benefit from support and external inspiration. An effective teacher can encourage you to transcend limitations, but no teacher is a substitute for the work you need to do.

Sometimes, students become insecure and self-critical when they haven't practiced enough. They tend to cancel lessons, reschedule or postpone learning. If you haven't gone to the gym in two weeks, is that a reason to say, "I shouldn't go today because I haven't been in a while?" One should go precisely *because* they haven't been practicing. If you fall off the wagon, get back on.

Diligent practice in conjunction with lessons will certainly yield results. Sporadic, infrequent, distracted practice is less effective. For this reason, crafting a routine is useful. Establishing days of the week and times of day to engage in a consistent routine enables practitioners to observe their development over time.

Think of it as a science experiment, operating on the hypothesis that, "if I practice, I will improve." The constant of the experiment is, "I will practice certain exercises for 10 minutes, twice a day, at 8:00 AM and 8:00 PM, for one month." These are the 'controls.' The 'variables' are your daily emotions, environmental factors, physical and mental states. Sometimes you'll be tired or discouraged, doubting your ability or whether the practice is producing beneficial results; at other times you'll be motivated and inspired. But no matter how you *feel*, the experiment must go on. Only then can you conclude if the practice routine has proven the hypothesis that, "if I practice, I will improve."

All kinds of excuses will try to come between you and your intentions, especially boredom, distraction and laziness. Don't pressure yourself to the point that all joy is sapped out of music, but *do* discipline yourself, and understand that long-term results are worth overcoming temporary discomfort. Learn to love the practice. Treat it as a meditation. The practice will evolve with you, as you are prepared to introduce variables. When you reach a plateau, it means you're ready for a new challenge. If you don't push your limits, your practice routine can become automatic and monotonous.

Nobody said mastery was easy. Attention to detail requires tremendous focus. Effortlessness is often the result of having put forth great effort to achieve it. Use your mind to set objectives and your willpower to accomplish them.

Just do what needs to be done.
Never take advantage of power.
Achieve results, but never glory in them.
Achieve results, but never boast.
Achieve results, but never be proud.
Achieve results, because this is the natural way.

— *Lao Tzu (Tao te Ching)*

Practicing with a *metronome* is highly recommended. A metronome is a musical clock. It reinforces frequency and consistency. If we couldn't rely on the sun rising and setting each day, how would we structure our time? If we can't count on ourselves to show up regularly to practice, how can we establish development? A metronome helps us meet the moment-to-moment deadlines of music.

When you have an appointment, you set the alarm. Public transportation depends on a time-table. Likewise, the beat of a metronome represents a series of rendezvous points between you and the music. If you're playing alone, it's ok to be loose and flowing, because time is truly flexible and fluid, but if you want to align with someone else, you'll need to share the sense of time. You must listen and respond to the other, not interrupt or fail to respond because you're lost somewhere else.

Training with a metronome results in rhythmic stability. This discipline is not confining, it is liberating. Without it, you only express half of the equation. You can be intuitive, free and flowing, but can you also be steady, clear, angular and well-defined? Many dancers practice with a metronome. Choreography (a 'graphic chorus') arranges a sequence of synchronized motions which require precision. Dance is essentially rhythmic; you have to move synchronistically to avoid 'stepping on each other's toes.' *Pranayama*, *qigong*, yoga *asanas* and *kriyas* also involve rhythmic processes. In our culture, the word 'discipline' is loaded with negative connotations. To some, it suggests severity, control and rigidity. However, the root of the word discipline is 'disciple.' In Latin, 'disciplina' means instruction or knowledge. When you become a disciple of sound, you enter into a deeper relationship. Through your own concerted effort, knowledge becomes accessible.

No one can make you a disciple. At some moment, if you are determined, you must take your relationship with sound and music to the level of discipleship. This inner drive for real knowledge will open doors for sound itself to instruct you in its mysteries. As you begin to speak the language of music, you will no longer require others to translate it for you. Rather, you will be able to converse more fluently with its elements. The library of the mysteries of sound are ever-present, ready to be heard and expressed.

The lips of wisdom are closed,
except to the ears of Understanding.

— Three Initiates (The Kybalion)

In order to learn, one must listen. Listen to yourself while you play, hear the sounds you produce and the silence you leave. Record yourself and play it back. Just as you listen to others, listen to yourself. Many people become mechanical. If musical choices are automatic or based on limited habits—

creativity suffers. Perhaps this is why people resist regimens and exercises—they fear losing creativity through conformity, becoming a slave to the metronome or the dogma of theoretical systems.

> *When the discipline doesn't lead to freedom,*
> *it's an imposition.*
> *All disciplines must lead to freedom.*
>
> *— Maestro Manuel Rufino*

Masculine and feminine principles of knowledge need to be balanced—giving and receiving, expressing and listening, pattern and chaos, sound and silence, determination and spontaneity, etc. It is possible to practice both constraint and reinvention. J.S. Bach's "Inventions" are sublime demonstrations of this. Using central themes, he crafted a series of variations that were playful and adventurous while operating within the logic of harmony as he heard it.

People habitually reinforce belief systems, physical postures and emotional attitudes throughout life. It's part of identity formation. By extension, groups of people construct cultural identities. To homogenize means 'to make of the same kind.' But homogeneity is not inherently bad, nor is it 'unmusical.' It produces uniformity, which is a principle of frequency. Discipline in music is not meant to establish limitations, but to increase one's flexibility with rhythm, melody, harmony, tone, theory and so on. This allows for creative self-expression with unlimited focus and clarity. Dominion over one's artistry is both liberating and empowering, and it requires highly developed technique. You are only as limited as your lack of practice and discipline.

11

Recorded Sound: Analog and Digital Signals

Humanity has two primary means of passing sonic information from one generation to the next. The first is oral history or aural transmission. The second is written or recorded history. Until very recently (the late 19th century), sound and music from the past could only be experienced through live interpretation. Performances kept the work of various composers and traditions alive. Historical instruments and techniques have been reproduced based on paintings and written descriptions. With the advent of recording technology, we are able to travel back in time and hear the voices of those who have passed.

What exactly are we hearing when we listen to recorded sound? How is sound recorded in the first place, and what is lost in translation from source to captured format and, ultimately, playback? This multi-stage process inevitably filters and distorts the original sonic content, but it also preserves it.

In one short century, humanity has contrived many means of recording sound. These can be organized in two fundamental categories:

1. Analog
2. Digital

Analog technology records the continuous mechanical energy of a sound wave. This has been accomplished using various devices—such as a crank-operated phonograph, which etches waveforms into a wax cylinder or disk—or the magnetic tape deck, which converts electrical signal into a magnetic field and then imprints it on a magnetizable strip of tape.

Digital sound requires electricity and signal conversion through a computer, giving rise to CD's, MP3's and other file formats. Binary code is used to convert analog signals into a language that is readable by a computer. This information can be written, read, erased and rewritten using laser optics and magnetic data storage, holographic drives, quantum computers and even DNA itself.[42]

Such broad definitions may leave the reader with more questions than answers. To that point, remember that these technologies require a deep understanding of physics, electrical engineering, computer science and mathematics. It is therefore beyond the scope of this book to examine the intricacies of analog and digital technology.

To better illustrate the point, the categories of analog and digital have parallels in film, which can be understood as light recording. The earliest cameras were analog, mechanical devices that relied on natural light and chemical processes to capture images. Eventually, electricity allowed for light-bulbs and digital cameras to interface with computers.

In the 20th century, as we learned to preserve audio, our relationship to sound and music changed drastically. Suddenly, we were able to document sound history and play it back. These technologies improved rapidly, and what began as grooves etched into wax, evolved into computer technologies that store virtually infinite quantities of information on magnetic disks. We even developed the capacity to beam these signals to outer space and back again.

Prior to recorded audio, music was experienced live, directly. People had to attend a performance or create music themselves if they wanted to hear it. The transition to recorded format had many impacts on our sonic diet. For one, early recordings could only last a few minutes, meaning that composers needed to reduce the scope of their work to fit within a brief time-frame. Long-form compositions, such as symphonies, couldn't be recorded without being segmented. This may have shortened listener attention spans over the course of decades, as popular culture was bombarded over radio and television by these standardized formats.

Of course, live sound never disappeared throughout this process. Performances continue to take place in performance halls, religious institutions, restaurants, bars, homes and other settings. However, as digital technology began to emerge, people increasingly turned to television, radio, DJ's, portable devices and internet-based streaming sources for their listening needs.

Ultimately, incorporating digital signal manipulation in sound and music allows us to create sonic environments which are irreplicable by an acoustic human voice or instrument. The computer has become an advanced musical instrument. Virtually all music produced in home studios, as well as for mainstream media, relies on computer technology.

The following are visual representations of analog and digital sine waves, respectively:

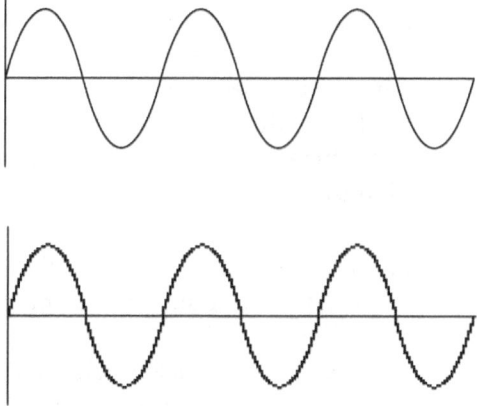

Top: Organic sine wave (analog)
Bottom: Binary sine wave (digital)

A basic principle of electricity and digital signals is that they turn on or off—current flows or is interrupted. These two states establish a binary structure. In computers, light bulbs (also known as pixels) are assigned 0 or 1 (on or off). An elaborate code is written to tell each bulb whether to light up or remain dark (intensity of brightness can also be assigned). A grid of bulbs can be programmed to represent a 'bitmap' image such as this:

A single image is called a frame. A series of images can be projected at a 'frame rate.' Film standards display between 24 and 60 frames per second, which fools the eye into thinking it is watching continuous motion when seeing a sequence of still images. In digital audio recording, the same concept is referred to as the 'sample rate.' In that sense, audio recording captures a series of 'sonic snapshots,' which are later played back at a rate that fools the ear into thinking it is hearing an unbroken sound signal (such as an industry standard 48 kHz, or 48,000 samples per second).

It is important to realize that, until recently, microphone technology was designed for the audible spectrum of the human ear (approximately 20 Hz – 20,000 Hz). This excludes non-audible frequencies that are nonetheless felt, or interact with us in other ways (as discussed in the chapter, "Experiencing the Unseen"). Recorded music is therefore biased to the ears and doesn't account for other equally important frequencies that interact with human perception. In other words, some of the sensitivity and depth of the experience are lost.

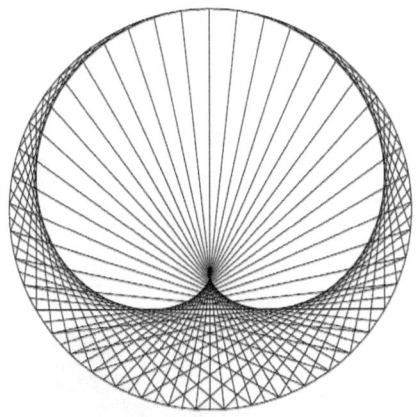

An image representing a 'cardioid' microphone polar pattern. Different microphones are designed to capture different frequency ranges and volumes and are considered to be 'directional.' Some frequencies and angles are perceived more strongly while others are rejected. Common polar patterns include 'cardioid,' 'omnidirectional' and 'figure-eight.'

Once an audio signal is captured, it can be modified in many ways. Pitch, tone, volume and tempo can all be adjusted—independently or in conjunction. But how is a signal captured in the first place? Sound can travel through any substance made of particles (air, wood, water, metal, etc.) but since we primarily hear sound travel through air, we will explore recording from this perspective.

Transduction is a fundamental principle of sound engineering. A transducer (literally 'to lead across') transforms energy from one form into another. Phonograph cylinder recording (patented by Thomas Edison in 1877) achieves this by funneling air through a large bell to a narrow point. This focused point of high pressure is strong enough to vibrate a metal diaphragm. A small stylus attached to this diaphragm records air pressure fluctuations by cutting into a wax cylinder which is rotated by a mechanical crank. In reverse, the stylus reads the wax grooves. These fluctuations are translated back into air pressure waves which are amplified through the bell of the device. As these air pressure waves strike your ear drum, sound is perceived through a neurological connection to the auditory system. In a sense, your auditory system transduces mechanical air pressure waves into vibrational signals which are then interpreted by your brain.

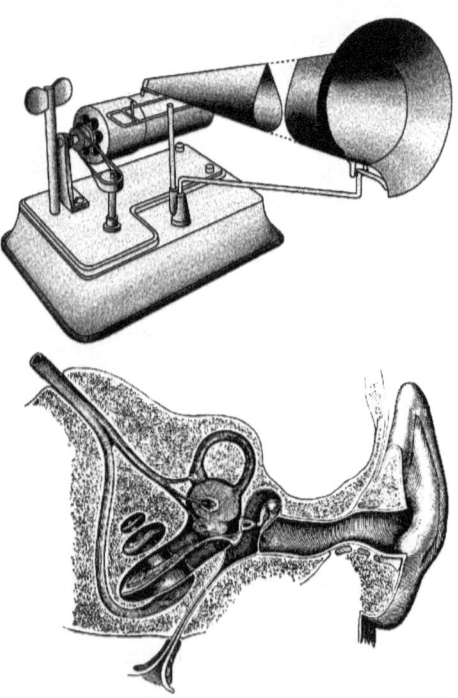

Many inventions are inspired by nature.

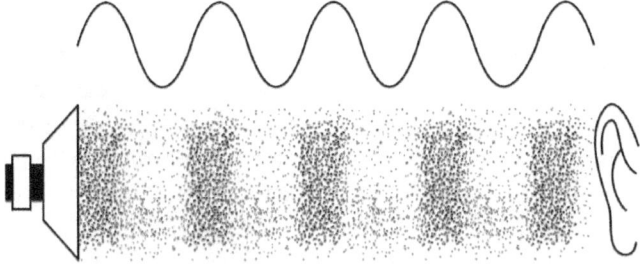

In the case of digital audio recording, air pressure waves are converted into an electrical signal. This electrical signal is later converted back into air pressure waves when played through a speaker. Microphones achieve transduction in various ways depending on their design. Some microphones use magnets and sensitive aluminum membranes to register minute fluctuations in air pressure. Others use crystals, carbon and various materials. However transduction is achieved, these fluctuations are recorded and imported into a computer where they can be read by a DAW (digital audio workstation), such as Logic or Ableton.

From there, complete signal manipulation is possible to the extent that the recording process was able to capture sonic information in the environment. With modern technology, any frequency bandwidth can be limited or enhanced to *equalize* or balance sounds on the recording. In general, frequencies are divided into *bass, middle* and *treble* ranges from low to high.

Digital effects such as reverb, delay, distortion, compression and phasing may also be added. Today, echolocation can be used to map the dimensions of a room. The sonic properties of the environment can then be emulated to create an artificial reverb that reproduces the auditory aesthetic of any environment, such as Madison Square Garden, a bathroom, cave or forest.

Dryness and wetness refer to the amount of unaffected and affected signals, respectively—in other words, how much of the effect is added.

More recently, pitch correction (auto-tune) and rhythmic *quantizing* have been used to align music to a strict mathematical grid. If a singer is out of tune, the sound engineer can isolate that note and change its frequency to the desired pitch. If a drummer hits the wrong beat, they can move it to another point in time. A digital drum loop is capable of infinitely repeating a mathematically precise beat, whereas a highly trained percussionist cannot sustain 'perfect' time endlessly. Likewise, a human being can only sing to the lung's capacity, whereas a synthesizer can sustain indefinitely.

There is virtually no aspect of recorded audio that cannot be manipulated by a computer. This has given birth to entire genres, such as electronic music and binaural beats, which can be constructed entirely from digitized sounds. In many cases, people listening to electronic music are not aware of what is human and what is computer-generated.

Images from a Digital Audio Work Station (DAW)

It is worth noting that an acoustic performance cannot be altered, whereas a digital recording can be endlessly remixed. Furthermore, amplified sound can be rendered exponentially louder or quieter than acoustic sounds. This requires a speaker.

Once an audio signal has been recorded and modified through a computer, it is ready to be reproduced through a speaker. Most speakers today operate by an electrical signal being sent through a metal coil, which interacts with a magnet to repel and attract. These compressions and rarefactions of the air amplify the signal through a speaker cone and dome to push the frequencies through space. High frequencies have short rapid wavelengths, while low frequencies have long slow wavelengths. Speaker sizes and power requirements can vary greatly based on the amount of what frequencies need to be produced. Whereas gramophones are powered by mechanical (crank and gear) energy, modern speakers rely on electric current to displace air.

Speaker Tweeter   *Speaker Cone*

Speakers come in many sizes and materials, but they are primarily based on the same principles. Speaker domes (also known as tweeters) are concave, whereas speaker cones are convex. The shape and size of a speaker affects its frequency response (what frequencies it is capable of reproducing), volume threshold and directionality.

Most humans have two ears; therefore, we are able to process stereo signals. Receiving inputs from multiple sources simultaneously creates a three dimensional perception of sound. Our eyes work similarly, with stereoscopic vision. Obviously, reducing our sensory input by half to a single eye or ear would be debilitating. Nevertheless, much of the world is listening to audio in 'mono' these days, meaning that sonic dimensionality is sacrificed. Most bluetooth speakers are essentially monophonic, since the sound source emanates from a central point, as opposed to stereo speakers placed in separate locations. Furthermore, they are compact, limiting frequency reproduction since current technology cannot generate a full audible spectrum through such underpowered, undersized devices.

On the other hand, modern advancements are bringing enhanced realism to the world of audio reproduction. Binaural audio achieves full 3D sound, as opposed to the left/right dichotomy of stereo. By placing microphones in a mold shaped like the human ear, sound engineers are able to capture sonic images that are closer to a true human listening experience. Ideally, an exact mold of your ears would be made, and microphones would be used to record audio customized especially for you, resulting in a recording that would sound very close to your natural hearing.

Binaural technology is great for immersive, spatially dynamic listening experiences. For instance, a 'binaural head' (two microphones positioned inside of a model human head) placed in the center of a symphony orchestra would result in a recording that reproduces what it would be like as a listener to be positioned there, while the same performance recorded from the back of the hall would produce a recording of the orchestra from that listening perspective. Within a digital ecosystem such as virtual reality, binaural recording can be used to great effect when programming lifelike simulations of auditory environments. For instance, a football game requires spatial accuracy, so a person knows where to look when their teammate calls.

Surround sound refers to various multi-speaker setups that add more dimension to the listening experience. Left—Center—Right is a three-speaker array, while Dolby 5.1 and 7.1 surround sound use five and seven speakers respectively (plus a subwoofer). Most recently, *spatial audio* expands on the idea by introducing an array of overhead speakers (see Dolby Atmos). If progress continues in this direction, we could imagine a listener suspended in space within a 'listening bubble.' Speakers would point at the listener from every possible direction, resulting in the most complete surround sound possible. With such a setup, sound engineers could mix audio to create motion above, below, to the center and all around.

While accurate reproduction of sound is a primary objective of recording, experimental manipulation of audio is another aspect of sound design, fabricating sonic textures we might never find in the 'natural' world. Electricity and digital music-making have pushed the limits of human expression to new frontiers, birthing what might be the most complex instrument ever invented—the computer.

From the prehistoric invention of the flute to the smelting of metal used to develop countless instruments, technology has always been part of human sound-making. External instruments allow us to make sounds we cannot produce with the body alone. Sometimes, the line between human and technology is gray. Recorded media has transformed the world immensely, with unforeseen impacts on the future of humanity. While this expands the musician's palette, it also presents the potential to entirely digitize the role of the artist.

The ability to manipulate pitch, volume, tone and speed means that—like air-brushing unwanted 'imperfections' from photographs of the human form—sound engineers can alter a live performance in post-production until it is aesthetically perfect according to subjective standards. This process of micro-managing art can be taken to any extreme. Part of the magic of a live performance is that it cannot be altered. It is spontaneous and unique. Once it is recorded, that performance may be mixed and re-mixed, but the original performance is the pure source.

12

CREATIVITY AND INSPIRATION

The names and the colors of the assorted species of beings
were all inscribed by the ever-flowing pen of God.
Who knows how to write this account? Just imagine
what a huge scroll it would take! What power! What
fascinating beauty! Who can know their extent?

— *Guru Nanak (Japji Sahib)*

Creativity is deeply important to all of us, especially those
who work with artistic forms of expression that involve
improvisation. Creativity is not an easy thing to define or
sustain throughout our lives. It touches every corner of life and
is connected to our physical, mental, emotional and spiritual
state of being. It responds to our empathic relationship with
others on an interpersonal and collective unconscious level. It
flows with the seasons, reflecting natural processes of turning
inward (winter), sewing and nurturing (spring), blooming and
producing (summer), fruiting and harvesting (fall).

Learning is one way to prevent stagnation and promote
creativity. Pick up a new instrument. Seek music you have never
heard before. Have conversations with people (whether they
identify as musicians or not) about sound and how it affects our
lives. Be open to unexpected connections and the benefits of
interdisciplinary research.

Do what inspires you, not only what you think you're 'supposed' to do. Sometimes we base our work on existing developmental models. We see what works for others and assume that if we apply it to our own lives, it will yield similar results. This can prevent us from finding creative solutions and approaches to self-expression.

Cultivate heart-connection, follow your intuition, and remember that the greatest source of inspiration may be where you least expect it: in nature, at a movie or play, in a book or an interaction with a stranger. Even heartache and suffering prove to be powerful sources of inspiration, peace and understanding when we creatively engage with the challenges we face.

When art exalts creation, inspiration is everywhere. Prayer and meditation help us acknowledge the benefit of being alive, to think well of others and be grateful. Art which seeks to defame others, claim superiority or dwell on materialism will reach the limits of what it can express. Fame and wealth are insatiable appetites, and creativity is exhausted in their pursuit. When self-expression parallels inner development, one's art will reflect an evolutionary process. Creativity allows us to express ourselves in healthy ways, through art and clear communication, rather than violence and vices.

> *The difference between culture and empire is that culture grows from within while empire grows from the outside, by taking in order to expand.*
>
> — *Maestro Manuel Rufino*

There are cycles in nature, just as there are periods of creativity juxtaposed with periods of integration and assimilation. Like the summers and winters of our lives, these periods are naturally fruitful or restful. It is important to remember in times of relative stagnation that seasons change—spring will come and renewed vitality will rush in to fill the space left by seemingly 'unproductive' periods. The principle of the empty cup is at play, reminding us that in order to be filled with inspiration, one must occasionally be devoid of it.

Contrast provides clarity.

Musical inspiration is a message received, a flower in bloom. It arises from nature and is not fabricated by the ego's desire to create. A work of art is the tip of an iceberg, emerging from one's inner world. A deep body of life experience gives form beneath the surface to the soul of an artist. These experiences influence what one has to express. A song is a focal-point which channels life experience into artistic expression or prayer. It is a highly concentrated synthesis of technique, feeling and meditation. A song distills the lesson learned, and shares that realization gained from experience. It is a peak moment, when the unconscious surfaces into expression. The act of expression is part of personal growth, as one creates art to move energy that might otherwise fester inside and contribute negatively to one's mental state.

A musician expands their capacity to receive and share musical messages by listening and meditating—and, from a technical perspective, by mastering the instruments and languages of music. In any case, music must be translated from the inside out. Music does not begin with the hands. An instrument is not an external object, it is an extension of oneself. At best, an instrument helps one express that music which exists within them. Technique involves mechanical as well as mental processes, whereby a person learns to transmit the vibrations of their entire being. This is how art interprets consciousness.

Sometimes, structure and limitation are great sources of creativity. Poetic forms such as the sonnet, sestina, haiku and villanelle follow strict rules that provide a framework in which to explore creativity. The paradox of restriction is reconciled by the infinite variation made possible through it. An hour cannot be shorter or longer than 60 minutes, but you may spend that hour any way you choose. Practicing technique and learning theory can be a mundane and tedious process, or it can be a liberating meditation. You decide.

Many artists are concerned with being unique. When you are natural, you see that no one is exactly like you. You are inherently original. Derivative art is the result of attempting to be or sound like someone else. It's worthwhile to emulate others in order to assimilate their techniques and expand your own palette, but not to lose yourself in the process.

Attempting to please others will conform you to popular taste. Of course we want to appeal to others, to be liked, to have our talents appreciated—but this is an unsustainable source of validation. Creativity depends on a willingness to break with norms and explore uncharted territory, regardless of the opinions of others.

Occasionally, novel instruments and technologies open new frontiers in music. Intercultural exchanges breed new genres (as in the case of jazz). However, pioneering approaches are often met with disdain. People are easily averse to that which they do not understand, taking it as a threat to what they prefer. Conversely, it can be discomforting to admit our own limitations and lack of exposure to cultures and concepts beyond our own. We often prefer to remain static and stick to what we know—a plateau of arrested development.

As soon as you catch yourself making a habitual choice, go left. Destabilize the mechanistic part of art and allow spontaneity to take the reins once in a while. What's the worst that can happen?

Throughout history, countless masterpieces have been lost and forgotten. Who knows how many artistic geniuses died in obscurity? You must be prepared to be the only witness of your heart. Creativity is between you and the Spirit. If someone recognizes you, great. If not, also great. Be great either way. Give it your all when no one is looking.

Countless silent sages, vibrating the strings of His love.
How can Your creative potency be described?

— Guru Nanak (Japji Sahib)

Remember, "there is nothing new under the sun."[43] Themes of love and loss are endlessly repeated in art from all times and places. They keep showing up in new clothes, but their essence remains the same. Creativity takes the same basic elements and finds infinite ways to combine them. In this sense, all art is derivative. Can you break entirely with your influences?

In Hinduism, *shakti* refers to the primal creative force. This force produces all forms, including our own physical bodies. Creation itself is the greatest teacher. Observe the many manifestations of nature; take inspiration from clouds, flowers, creatures and the elements. The world around us is endlessly inventive. Observe this effortless wisdom and participate in the process. You are not merely *of* creation, you *are* a creator.

13

Mastery

The wise musicians are those who play what they can master.
— Duke Ellington

My teacher reminds me, "If you want to teach, learn. And if you want to learn, teach." We are always teaching and learning. These are twin states of a single relationship.

There is always a lesson hidden in plain sight. Can birds teach you to sing? Can the wind teach you to breathe calmly? What can you learn about melody from a river? What rhythms can you hear in the passing clouds?

The way to mastery is to humble oneself, to look into what one does not know and therefore come to understand (to *stand under*). One must occasionally bow to the knowledge of others. Many have dedicated their lives to penetrating great mysteries. We are fortunate to receive their legacies through written and recorded materials—aural teachings and examples of embodied mastery.

Mastery is a process of integration. It is not enough simply to have a vision of how great you can be. Of course the overgrown lawn *could* become a vegetable garden, but only if you acquire the tools, work the land, sew the seeds and tend the crop can you harvest the fruits of labor. Growth requires a concerted effort.

People are natural, intuitive artists—but developing technique and sensitivity with practice, study and deep listening can enhance self-expression. Knowledge can be acquired through emulation, as a child learns by following the example of peers and elders. It can also be acquired with guidance from a master.

Some people are reluctant to receive a teacher's instruction. They may fear stifling their creative freedom by submitting to a disciplined course of study. They may even, out of ignorance or arrogance, scorn the formal training of others. My own teacher refers to this impulsive rejection as the attitude of an, "automatic rebel."

> *Only a fool can dedicate themselves*
> *to teach somebody who already knows.*
>
> — *Maestro Manuel Rufino*

The ethos of punk music captures something of this non-conformist approach to music itself. Still, the distinct rawness of the genre owes something to its self-made pioneers, as do the legacies of blues, jazz and hip hop. There is much to be said in support of the autodidactic approach, yet the models of conservatory education and the master-disciple relationship have clearly produced and preserved precious lineages of tradition.

There is inevitably some tug-of-war between the old and new generations. Innovators must somehow differentiate themselves from the past and therefore transcend the paradigms of the time. Perhaps the greatest risk of submitting to a master is enslaving oneself to dogma. But respecting a master is very different from idolizing or copying them religiously. The student who is a blind follower will never achieve originality. A wise pupil develops insight through experimentation—actively exploring, dissecting and applying teachings, rather than formulaically regurgitating them.

If you follow in the footsteps of a master, you become a shadow. There are teachers who can teach us things we need to know and integrate into our lives to make us better people, but a guru is not one that you follow. A guru is a dispeller of evil.

— *Oh Shinnah (Profiles in Wisdom)*

Some struggle with inferiority, perceiving others to be superior to them simply because they are more accomplished in a particular way. Each of us exhibits strength and weakness. Mastery plays to one's strengths to overcome limitations. This requires dedication and determination, and a willingness to face one's actual competence. Therefore, mastery brings both confidence and humility.

If the universe is a university, there is no end to growth and learning. One can always improve technique, learn more songs or go deeper into the nuances of interpretation. Mastery is not a plateau to reach or a pinnacle of greatness. It is a way of being which rises continuously to the obstacles and opportunities of life. In that sense, we're all improvising.

It is impossible to be exactly like someone else. If we attempt to embody our heroes, we inevitably disembody ourselves. Likewise, no one can be exactly like you. You have innate, irreplicable beauty. To that effect, a master is a mirror, reflecting the qualities we wish to cultivate in ourselves. A master is in harmony, balanced, understanding and inspired, with the will and discipline to bring visions into reality—to birth a masterpiece.

Excuses are obstacles you put to your own freedom.

— *Maestro Manuel Rufino*

*Deceiving oneself, leads us down a wrong path
that ends in a desert of suffering and disharmonies.*

— *Maestro Domingo Dias Porta*

There are many paths to mastery, whether by the time-tested rigors of tradition or an unprecedented call of inspiration. In either case, the responsibility of attaining mastery rests squarely on the shoulders of the individual.

14

CLOSING REMARKS

You are in motion, on your way to resolving the past, coming into harmony with present conditions and exercising your capacity to consciously affect the future. The vibrations that constitute 'you' are aligned to this purpose. You can identify vibrations of love as readily as those of anger or sadness. You can invoke and project peace. You can feel the impact each nutrient has on your state of being as it is processed by your system. You recognize thoughts which lead to angst and negativity as well as those which lead to creative solutions. You feel the benefits of a breath of fresh air, a warm smile in the sunshine, a purifying immersion in the sea.

While you experience these things, although they temporarily absorb your focus, you are not defined by them.

Each vibration comes and passes. They are sensations experienced *by* you, and although they do contribute to your identity, they are not the essence of what you are. In this body, you experience likes and dislikes, tastes and preferences, ways and particularities. You are not attached to them. You are not ultimately defined by them. Your function transcends your form.

No longer caught in the illusion of the merely external, you respect your inner temple. You recognize that place where no eye can penetrate, no foreign mind can access and no prison can be constructed but the one you impose on yourself. No one can tell you what you must discover for yourself. Integrated knowledge is not in books. Beauty is not in appearances. Love is not in the words or actions of another.

This understanding comes with responsibility, and taking responsibility leads to freedom from the unwanted effects of unconscious causes.

You hold the reins of self-realization. Now that you have undertaken to perceive how all vibrations rise and fall, how they run their course, you have set yourself to the task of observing deeply even the subtlest aspects of life. Every gear in the watch is essential. Every leaf on the tree is vital. No interconnection can be overlooked if things are to be properly harmonized, synchronized and aligned. When there is peace in you, there is peace in the world.

Life is not a prison. It is a sandbox. If anything unifies the cosmos, it is energy, and energy vibrates. By vibration you are created, and by vibration you create. Mastering these forces, you can harness the energies of life and direct them by will towards the manifestation of the highest good.

Notes

1. Declared by King Solomon thousands of years ago in the philosophical masterpiece *Ecclesiastes*.

2. Strain, George M. "How Well Do Dogs and Other Animals Hear?" Frequency Hearing Ranges in Dogs and Other Species

3. Hermes Trismegistus. *The Emerald Tablet*. Evanescent Press

4. Yogananda, Paramahansa. *Autobiography of a Yogi*. Self-Realization Fellowship

5. Khan, Hazrat Inayat. *The Mysticism of Sound and Music*. Shambhala

6. Kandaswamy, Rajalakshmi. "Application of Sound Frequencies as an Epigenetic Tool in Reversing the Limiting Symptoms of Autism." *IMedPub*

7. Frost, Gavin. Frost, Yvonne. *Astral Travel: Your Guide to the Secrets of Out-of-The-Body-Experiences.* Samuel Weiser

8. Rollin, McCraty, et al. "The Electricity of Touch: Detection and Measurement of Cardiac Energy Exchange between People." *HeartMath Institute*, Laurence Erlbaum Associates

9. See the work of Ernst Chladni, pioneering researcher of acoustics.

10. Hans, Jenny. Cymatics: A Study of Wave Phenomena & Vibration (3rd ed.). Macromedia Press. 2001

11. Lenshof, Andreas. "Acoustophoresis." *SpringerLink*

12. Science World. "Sound = Vibration, Vibration, Vibration". *Science World*

13. HeartMath. "HeartMath Science | HeartMath Institute." *HeartMath Institute*

14. See also the experimental work of John Stuart Reid's *Cymascope*.

15. Kenyon, Tom. "Theoretical Constructs of ABR Technology". *Tom Kenyon*

16. NASA. "Lightning Strike: Speed of Sound." *NASA*

17. US Department of Commerce, National Oceanic and Atmospheric Administration. "How Far Does Sound Travel in the Ocean?" *NOAA's National Ocean Service*

18 Bhatia, Aatish. "The Loudest Sound Ever Heard." *Discover Magazine*

19. Classic Fm. "Listen to the eerie, real-life sounds of every planet in our solar system." Classic Fm

20. For an in-depth exploration of circadian rhythms and other biological processes, see: Gaer Lucy, Gay "Biological Rhythms in Human and Animal Physiology." Dover Pubns

21. Woodford, Chris. "How Quartz Watches and Clocks Work." *Explain That Stuff*

22. Nelson, Jon. "What Is an Atomic Clock?" *NASA*

23. Nace, Trevor. "Quartz Coin Can Hold 360 TB of Data for Billions of Years." *Forbes*

24. Baconnier, Simon, et al. "Calcite Microcrystals in the Pineal Gland of the Human Brain: First Physical and Chemical Studies." *Bioelectromagnetics, vol. 23, no. 7*

25. US EPA, OCSPP. "What Is the Endocrine System? | US EPA." *US EPA*

26. The term 'inner negative belief' is borrowed from *The Possible You* seminar created by Rabbi Yom Tov Glaser. There are many programs and approaches to inner engineering that incorporate elements of repatterning, such as the *Landmark Forum*, *Alcoholics Anonymous* and *Vipassana* meditation, among others. All of these highly structured methods are effective in part because they establish time-ordered

frameworks in which to practice and apply techniques for rewiring habitual behaviors.

27. Gareth Cook. "Does Consciousness Pervade the Universe?" *Scientific American*

28. See *The Yoga Sutras of Patanjali*, *Raja Yoga* by Swami Vivekenanda and *Light on Pranayama* by B.K.S. Iyengar for detailed explanations.

29. Mayo Clinic Staff. "Meditation: A simple, fast way to reduce stress." *Mayo Clinic*

30. MasterClass "How to Practice Dhyana: A Guide to the Seventh Limb of Yoga." *MasterClass*

31. HeartMath "The Science of HeartMath." *HeartMath*

32. Johnson, M.W.; Richards, W.A.; Griffiths, R.R. "Human hallucinogen research: guidelines for safety." *Journal of Psychopharmacology*

33. Kim, Yoo Yung. "Teasing the Science behind Brain Tingles in ASMR." *Psychology Today, Sussex Publishers*

34. Solomon, Robert. "Racism and Its Effect on Cannabis Research." *Cannabis and Cannabinoid Research, vol. 5, no. 1*

35. See Campbell, Don. *The Mozart Effect: Tapping the Power of Music to Heal the Body, Strengthen the Mind, and Unlock the Creative Spirit.* Avon Books

36. See *Yug, Yoga, Yogismo* by Dr. Serge Reynaud de La Ferriere for a thorough exploration of chakra science.

37. Winkler, Gershon. *Magic of the Ordinary: Recovering the Shamanic in Judaism.* North Atlantic Books

38. Center for Non-Destructive Evaluation. "Nondestructive Evaluation Physics:Sound." *Center for Non-Destructive Evaluation*

39. Baconnier, Simon, et al. "Calcite Microcrystals in the Pineal Gland of the Human Brain: First Physical and Chemical Studies." *Bioelectromagnetics, vol. 23, no. 7*

40. ReFaey, Karim, et al. "The Eye of Horus: The Connection between Art, Medicine, and Mythology in Ancient Egypt." *Cureus*

41. Graff-Radford, Jonathan. "Can Music Help Someone with Alzheimer's?" *Mayo Clinic*

42. Church, George. et. al. "Next-Generation Digital Information Storage in DNA." *Science Express. Department of Genetics, Harvard University.*

43. From the book of *Ecclesiastes.*

About the Author

Adrian DiMatteo (B.M. Eastman School of Music, 2012) is the founder of the Sonic Institute. He is an international performing and recording artist, author, music educator, app creator (Chord Atlas), and sound meditation facilitator with over 20 years' experience in the music world. Adrian has traveled extensively—exploring sound, language, musical culture and how they affect individual and collective wellbeing. Adrian regularly facilitates Sound Healer Training programs and retreats. To date, he has offered musical experiences to thousands of people in hospitals, hospices, elder care facilities, prisons, and children's centers.

SONIC
INSTITUTE

sonicinstitute.com

info@sonicinstitute.com